Life, Love, Lies & Lessons

A Journey through Truth to find an Authentic Life

Sharon Pope

Copyright © 2014 Sharon Pope.

All rights reserved. No part of this book may be used or reproduced by any means, graphic, electronic, or mechanical, including photocopying, recording, taping or by any information storage retrieval system without the written permission of the publisher except in the case of brief quotations embodied in critical articles and reviews.

Balboa Press books may be ordered through booksellers or by contacting:

Balboa Press
A Division of Hay House
1663 Liberty Drive
Bloomington, IN 47403
www.balboapress.com
1 (877) 407-4847

Because of the dynamic nature of the Internet, any web addresses or links contained in this book may have changed since publication and may no longer be valid. The views expressed in this work are solely those of the author and do not necessarily reflect the views of the publisher, and the publisher hereby disclaims any responsibility for them.

Any people depicted in stock imagery provided by Thinkstock are models, and such images are being used for illustrative purposes only. Certain stock imagery © Thinkstock.

Printed in the United States of America.

ISBN: 978-1-4525-8987-9 (sc)
ISBN: 978-1-4525-8988-6 (hc)
ISBN: 978-1-4525-8986-2 (e)

Library of Congress Control Number: 2014900468

Balboa Press rev. date: 1/13/2014

For Derrick

I love your open, loving, authentic heart.

Contents

Acknowledgments ix
Introduction xi

Love Lessons in Truth 1

Chapter 1   The Creation of Lonely 3
Chapter 2   The Truth 11
Chapter 3   Playing with Fire 17
Chapter 4   Reflections of Brokenness 23
Chapter 5   You're off the Hook 27
Chapter 6   In Love with Possibility 33
Chapter 7   My Heart 37
Chapter 8   Affection and Connection 43
Chapter 9   Expectations 49
Chapter 10 It's Always about Us 53
Chapter 11 The Test 59
Chapter 12 Vulnerability Is Not a Four-Letter
               Word (But Control Should Be!) 65
Chapter 13 Honor and Cherish 73
Chapter 14 Love 77

Life Lessons in Truth 85

Chapter 15 Here I Am 87
Chapter 16 Next, Next, Next 93
Chapter 17 The Voice 97
Chapter 18 Sometimes I Scare Myself 103
Chapter 19 New Neighbors 111
Chapter 20 The Glorification of Busy 117
Chapter 21 Get Real 125
Chapter 22 The Mirror and the Demons 131
Chapter 23 Courage 139
Chapter 24 Light 145

Chapter 25	Still	151
Chapter 26	Bubble Wrap	159
Chapter 27	Enlightenment	165
Chapter 28	Faith	171
Chapter 29	Angels	179
Chapter 30	Authenticity	187

Epilogue 191

Acknowledgments

My deepest and most loving gratitude for the Daughters of the King:

> Traci Snyder, Julie Hatch, Cyndi Stayrook, Amy Bixel, Angelyn Atha and Donna Nolan.

For those that have encouraged and inspired me, I am humbled by your presence in my life:

> Jason Krauss and House of Krauss, Antonio Smith, Mike Sayre, Tim & Lisa Barrett, Trainer Sue Markovitch, Grayson Atha, Tracey Carruthers, Kathy Houck and Donna Wiles.

Thank you, Mom and Dad, for your quiet and steadfast strength.

For eleven years, Jason.

For all the teachers I have had and the lessons you have taught me. Some lessons were more difficult to endure than others, but all of them helped shape this path to truth, and for that, I am eternally grateful.

Gratitude and praise for The One who placed the desire to write in my heart and who guides my path and watches over me each day.

Introduction

You are God's crowning accomplishment. You are a unique and beautiful creation of God. No one in all of history has ever been you, and no one will ever be again. You are one of a kind. You have a story to tell that no one else can tell. If you do not tell it, it will never be heard, and someone needs to hear it! It doesn't have to be a story of drama or heroism. It only has to be real and honest.

I was in the middle of writing this book the day I received this note of encouragement through an e-mail from my church pastor, Linda Middelberg. She didn't know that I was writing a book. She didn't know that it had been in the works for more than two years and that I was lacking the inspiration I needed to finish the project. Although she knew the broad brushstrokes of my life, she didn't know the details of my struggles over the years or the complete transformation I experienced in order to become the person she knows today. She sent this e-mail to many people who received her daily sources of inspiration, but for so many reasons I claimed it as my own, as if she had only sent it directly to me, for me.

This is a simple story of how truth can transform a woman's life. My darkest hours were the catalyst for my brightest days. The hardest lessons I needed to endure led to my greatest blessings. There's growth in times of heartache and struggle. I believe that I now feel gratitude at a deeper level, because I know what it feels like to have lost something or someone. I now know what real joy feels like after experiencing profound sadness. Every challenge contains a lesson if we're open enough to learning from it. It takes some honesty and courage to move through those times, to heal the wounds and not get stranded there in the pain. But I'm living proof that it's possible.

I had been living a numb existence of a life for many years. I got married at age twenty-seven to a nice man of the same age. I had a good job, steadily and aggressively moving up the corporate ladder as fast as I could, I was active in my church, sitting on nearly every committee there was, one at a time. I exercised regularly, spent time with my family, cooked and baked for others, had cookouts with the neighbors, and loved to entertain; I had a four-bedroom house in the suburbs, a large circle of friends, one dog, no children, a 401(k), and a pension. And I believed that what I had created for my life was enough, in fact more than enough. I had no excuses not to be happy; so why wasn't I?

To face some of my own truths, I had to be broken open to the point of surrender, to where I had no other choice but to face my fears and heal some wounds. What I found along the way was a life that was genuinely my own and a soul that I could view in the mirror each day. I am not proud of all my choices, but this story is wholly mine—the good, the bad, the blessed, the sad, the outrageous, the trying, the joy and the crying, the gratitude, the love and the peace … all of it. These are the stories of the journey through a transformation to finding my authentic self—the woman I was meant to be, the woman who had been hidden for so long, the woman God calls me to be today. It is the story and lessons of how I learned to love myself, forgive myself, and be true to myself. It is the story and lessons of the people that have been brought into my life to teach me and transform me and to create a life worth sharing.

It is also your story. Not all of it, of course, but pieces of it. We all have wounds to heal—every single one of us. If you don't have some emotion, some insecurity, some misdeed, some habit or characteristic that you'd rather the world not know about you, then I'm sorry, but you also don't have a pulse. Everyone has some degree of darkness that could use a little brightness. As poet Charles Bukowski once wrote, "We must bring our own light to the darkness," so that's where the journey begins.

I have some core beliefs and truths that will become apparent.

> I believe your relationships with others—with your family, your friends, your partner, your weight, your money, and your work—are really just mirror images of the relationship that you have with yourself. Therefore, you have to heal yourself first.

> I believe we all wear a mask to some degree: some will do it through excess weight as the physical manifestation of hiding the darkness that's inside, while some will hide who they are by losing themselves in their children and family or job, so that there's nothing left for themselves. My mask of choice was my unique ability to appear as though I had it all together, all the time.

> I believe that God has been at work in my life all along, as I believe He is in yours. He never promised it would be easy; He doesn't always give us what we want, when we want it; but I know that every time I thought I knew, He showed me that I didn't. And when I thought surely He would give up on me, He did not. I am no minister and am certainly not qualified to teach others about God's love, so you won't see any Bible verses in this book. All I can do is share with you my experience of how God's love impacted my journey.

I believe that we all are enough. All those voices in our heads that try to hold us back by telling us that we're not good enough, smart enough, skinny enough, or talented enough are noise. If we can get to a place of stillness, that noise will quiet, and we will be able to hear our own inner voices and feel our own inner wisdom. We will find the voices, beauty, talent, intelligence, and grace that are alive and well in each of us.

I believe that we're all here to help one another, and I hope that in some small way this helps you along your path and propels you forward to find an open, honest, authentic life for yourself. Doing so takes courage (to go to some dark places and ask yourself some difficult questions), self-awareness (to be honest about who you are and who you are not), and self-love (to be patient and forgiving of yourself in the process). It's not easy, but there is only one way through this forest, and I've always believed in the light on the other side.

I believe that every woman has a journey to authenticity that is all her own, but most of us are too scared to wade into the deep end because the fear of drowning is too great. It's a process without shortcuts, so be gentle with yourself along the way. Because it is impossible to live simultaneously in both peace and denial, this journey requires us to commit to facing the truth and that which is real, learning from all the people and experiences, the angels and the demons. It is a journey to find and forgive ourselves. It is a journey to peace and authenticity. It is a journey to our own hearts.

Let's begin.

Love Lessons in Truth

The most beautiful people we have known are those who have known defeat, known suffering, known struggle, known loss, and have found their way out of the depths. These persons have an appreciation, a sensitivity, and an understanding of life that fills them with compassion, gentleness, and a deep loving concern. Beautiful people do not just happen.
—Elisabeth Kübler-Ross

CHAPTER 1

The Creation of Lonely

We are all designed to live through something
and that thing was designed to change us.
—Donald Miller

In hindsight and to everyone around me, it appeared as though my life had changed in an instant; but of course it had not.

I was the young, assertive woman who always had things under control and always knew where she was headed. After dating men, through my early twenties, who had lied or cheated, I decided that I wanted a good man. I chose Jason. We met in graduate school; I thought he looked like a banker. In fact, he was working for a bank at the time. He was six feet tall, clean-cut with short, dark hair—so short that people often thought he was in the military. He was smart, needing to get an A in every one of his graduate classes so that he could graduate with nothing less than a 4.0. He was structured and disciplined, but not in a strict, narrow-minded way. He was the middle child of divorced parents who harbored no resentment toward the breakup of their marriage. Jason worked hard and was tidy at home and frugal as the day was long. He exercised often, liked to watch college and pro football, packed his lunch, starched and ironed his clothes the night before work, got to bed early, paid the bills, followed the rules, and said "please" and "thank you." He was simple and kind; he was and is a good man with a kind heart.

Unfortunately, he didn't stand a chance.

I sought him out in our graduate school classes, paying attention to where he said he hung out on the weekends; I went out of my way to be at a place where I thought I would run into him. I approached him. I knew early in our relationship that this was the man I was going to marry—he wouldn't lie to me or cheat on me or leave me; he wouldn't hurt me. I was going to make this one work. Period.

One year into our dating relationship, he hadn't yet told me that he loved me. So, like any good, controlling woman worth her salt, I gave him an ultimatum. I said that if he didn't love me after a year of being together that maybe he never would and that he had a decision to make (as if a decision of the heart could or should be left to the mind, much less a driven woman with a plan). He very quickly acquiesced and told me he loved me, and not long after, we were engaged. I began molding our lives together and creating the shell that would be our marriage.

I planned every aspect of our lives: the wedding details, the house, the furniture, where we vacationed, where we would go out to eat or what movie we would see, what kind of dog we would get and when we would get her. I decided who our primary friends were, what color we would paint every room in the house, and what meals would be served for dinner over and over and over again. I planned our social calendar. I didn't nag my husband; I didn't have to. Rarely did Jason make a decision without seeking my opinion in advance.

I was busy moving quickly through life, always trying to get to what was next and very rarely stopping to enjoy the present. I was exceptional at leading everyone around me to believe that I was fine. I was more than fine. I had this thing called life *together* (insert smirk here). I had all the things I was supposed to have at this stage in my life. I did what I was supposed to do, or at least what everyone expected me to do. I showed up but wasn't particularly engaged or interested in anyone's life—including my own; I was simply too busy to be bothered with the details that come along with being genuinely involved in the lives of those around me. I hid my own fears and insecurities behind a veil of sarcasm. It served as a shortcut to be able to get my point across in an indirect way (some might call it a passive-aggressive way), rather than having direct, honest, open, loving conversations. I didn't have the time, the luxury, or the courage to confront my own weaknesses or my own fears. I felt that if I ever exposed those feelings, someone else might also see that my life wasn't picture perfect. The thought of showing weakness or letting my insecurities come to the surface was literally unthinkable to me.

My life was hollow, void of any purpose or passion. I was empty. I was angry. I was sad. I was lonely. My prayer during this time was, "God, do you see me?"

I thought the husband, home, nice car, golden retriever, good job, and retirement plan was what I had always wanted and would provide me the happy life I had always envisioned. So why was I so lonely?

Lylah Alphonse, the senior editor of *Manage Your Life*, wrote an article in 2011 entitled, *"Are You Stuck in a Semi-Happy Marriage?"* She defined a semihappy marriage as one of "low conflict, low passion, and low satisfaction." I guess that's as good a description as any of how I viewed my marriage at that time.

There was no passion in Jason's life or my own. I don't blame him; that is the man that I met, the man I dated for almost three years, and the same man that I ultimately married, with whom I spent more than a decade. We loved each other, but we were never lovers. I truly didn't even know what that word meant at the time.

We loved each other, but we were never lovers.

We did not cuddle, caress, lose time together; not once did he come up behind me while I was working in the kitchen, put his hands around my waist, and kiss my neck. Not once did I wake up to his arms wrapped tightly around me. As a matter of fact, I wasn't allowed to even touch him while he slept, lest he be awakened. The same walls I built around myself seemed to have followed me into my bed. Not once did he refer to me as beautiful or stunning, although I would occasionally be told that I was cute or pretty. I did not feel safe with him or protected by him or "taken care of." I'm not sure he would fight for me or defend me even if I was in trouble. If I was stressed, he never just said, "I've got you," or, "I've got this," and take care of things. We never made love for hours on end, stopping only to catch our breath or look into each other's eyes and whisper, "I love you." We very rarely fought. The only thing we had serious, consistent discussions about was the lack of affection in our relationship; I wanted it, and he wasn't comfortable giving it.

As time went on and my heart opened more, I began asking for love and affection from Jason. Over the years the requests became more frequent and the urging on my part more emotional; I wanted the kind of love that I saw in others. I recall going to a comedy club one night with some other couples and missing part of the show because I was so distracted by the simple, easy affection one couple was sharing. During the show they were sitting close together; he had his hand draped over her knee with his fingers wrapped around the inside of her leg. She was leaning back and had her arm around the back of his chair, touching his shoulder, occasionally placing her hand on the back of his head with her fingers gently in his hair. It was relaxed, simple, easy, and genuine. I sat there mesmerized by it, getting a bit too lost in it. Don't get me wrong; this couple didn't have a relationship that I envied. But then why was I so enamored with the ease with which they were able to express their love?

Please understand that my husband loved me and wanted to meet my needs, but it simply wasn't in him to give. He comes from a long lineage of unaffectionate men. He did try and would have kept trying for a lifetime. He hadn't changed; I had. Along this journey I realized that what I wanted simply wasn't within him to give, and so I stopped asking.

That realization changed the trajectory of my life. I knew I had to learn to live without passion and affection, and I was trying to make peace with that reality. I tried to focus on all the good that Jason had inside him, and on making that be enough for me. If I could have told him, instructed him—maybe given him a list of what I needed each day—in how to make me happy, to help me feel secure, loved, and adored, to fill that hole in me, he would have pulled out that list faithfully and tried to check every box, every day. But I couldn't do that, because I didn't know exactly what it should look like either, and I had grown tired of asking. Not surprisingly, the distance between us became greater. It wasn't just the lack of affection or the distance that was being created; it was also this empty, superficial life I had created that left me with little joy, connection, or direction.

I walked out on my marriage the Sunday evening of Thanksgiving weekend. I packed my bags that afternoon, while Jason was out, and when he came home, I told him I was leaving. I didn't give him much of an explanation; I don't think I had one. I can't even remember what I said, but I remember that day, that sadness and that anxiety, very clearly. He knew something had been wrong with me recently, and I think he thought I was just being dramatic. I don't think it sank in for him until a day or two later, when I didn't return home. He was hurt, badly. Six months later, our divorce was final.

Love Lesson in Truth

Looking back on the steady collapse of my marriage, I found several truths that serve me well today and lead me to greater love. Relationships and people are not stagnant; they grow and they evolve—sometimes in the same direction, sometimes in different directions. We shouldn't be so surprised by it; rather, we should come to expect it. Although I communicated to my husband about one element of our marriage—the lack of affection—I couldn't articulate or demonstrate for either of us what that could look like or feel like for two people who had never really known affection or intimacy in either of their lives.

When you pledge your life to someone, you're committing to being open and honest through that journey. You're committed to supporting them as they grow and change and evolve into a better human being, and the best possible version of themselves. I didn't live up to my end of that commitment. My divorce was the most profound change I've ever gone through, but it was the catalyst for the most massive growth period I could have ever imagined.

My greatest learning, however, was more about the life that I had created for myself. I was controlling, distant, and wearing my mask of "I got this," with great pride. If there was a way to earn a black belt in control, I would have been a controlling ninja! I had built up an enormous wall around me that was nearly impossible for anyone to scale: not my husband, not my family, not my coworkers, and not most of my friends. I had created that empty life, and the person I have to blame for this is the same person who stares back at me in the mirror each morning. Pride and arrogance were my ingredients for a pretty miserable heart. I didn't love myself very much; therefore, I didn't love anyone else very much either. Allowing someone else to know me and to love me was a mirror that I simply wasn't ready to face yet. Radical responsibility and brutal honesty were the tools that brought me out, brought me through, and eventually showed me love.

CHAPTER 2

The Truth

If you want to get to the castle ...
you've got to swim the moat.
—Elizabeth Gilbert, *Eat, Pray, Love*

One common theme you will hear throughout this journey of mine is that just when I think I've got it all figured out, I am humbled again and again with the simple fact that I do not.

> Just when I think I've got it all figured out, I am humbled again and again with the simple fact that I do not.

During our separation, I very naively thought that I could deal with this one element of my life—the absolute ruin of my marriage—isolate it from everything else, simply address it and move on without impacting any other part of my life. I could swiftly move onto becoming more, achieving more. I could continue, with all other elements of my life not being impacted at all: not my work, not my friends or family, certainly not who I was. I was in such denial about the severity of what was taking place that when I left to move into temporary housing, the random items I thought most important to bring along with me, outside of the obvious clothes, shoes, and toiletries, were linen napkins, charger plates, gift wrap, and my KitchenAid mixer. I'm not sure who I thought I was going to be hosting a dinner party for; those days were gone for a while. I was thinking this was a minor outpatient procedure, when it was really open heart surgery.

Leaving my husband and subsequently going through a divorce impacted every single aspect of my life: it shook my confidence, tested my faith, made me worse at my job, and impacted every relationship I had with both family and friends. Family was confused and, although they wanted to help, they didn't know how—so they were quietly supportive. Our mutual friends felt like they had to choose sides and couldn't possibly be friends with both my ex-husband and me. Because I was the one who initiated this and therefore placed them in such a precarious position, it was I who lost a good number of our mutual friends. I was unable to focus at work—a result of not sleeping much, drinking entirely too much, and nursing a repeatedly broken heart (stay tuned). This experience shook the core of who I was, but, frankly, I needed a little shaking up.

Most women don't live in a castle (or anything close to it).

Most women don't feel happy, content, or fulfilled in their lives (as sad as that is).

Most women don't feel secure (so we attempt to control everything around us).

Most women don't feel hopelessly, completely devoted to anyone (outside of their children).

Most women don't feel beautiful, fabulous, or stunning (but we all are in our own ways).

I wanted that. I wanted to be in the infinitely small percentage of women that had that kind of fulfillment in their lives and relationships. And I was willing to work and wait for it. Up until this point, as long as I was willing to work hard, I had always gotten what I wanted in life. I thought I'd just work hard and would ultimately get what I want. I wanted what I called "big love." I didn't want the ordinary, everyday, semi-happy love.

We can't isolate one part of our lives—certainly not something as central as marriage—fix it, and move on. The collapse of any marriage is caused by something much greater that we admit to initially, and that thing that is broken permeates and infects, not just the marriage, but all other aspects of life as well.

When I look back on my married life, I don't like myself very much. I was unhappy, distant, full of self-doubt, and fearful. I wasn't real; I certainly wasn't living an honest, authentic life. I put up a facade for everyone around me. I didn't recognize or embrace my own heart and therefore never let anyone in too far, for fear of what they might see. I also avoided meaningful conversations that might allow me the privilege to really know others.

There were probably hundreds of occasions where we had invited family over to our home to share a meal together. During those times, you would find me in the kitchen being busy preparing the meal. Even during dinner I always had something in the oven, dishes to clear from the table, a dessert to prepare, a dog to monitor. I kept myself busy to avoid sitting across from someone and being fully present in that moment. I was so fearful of being seen myself, that I never truly wanted to see anyone else. I was critical of others, even family members (particularly his family). I kept moving, kept striving, kept reaching—without even knowing what I was reaching for or whom I had left behind in the process. What a sad existence.

None of that, by the way, had anything to do with my husband or his family. That was all me. Therefore, it was mine to heal.

Love Lessons in Truth

I didn't know who I was. I didn't recognize my own heart. I couldn't have picked it out of a lineup if I had to. And I didn't like myself very much. So how could I possibly open myself up and share who I really was with anyone else? This created an unspoken but understood barrier between me and virtually everyone else in my life. It was easier for me to sit there behind my wall in my sadness than to admit it, face it, and heal it. I needed to discover who I was—in a relationship, out of a relationship, in my career, in my friendships, in my own skin.

We bring our whole selves to a relationship. If we're broken, our partners feel that brokenness, even if they can't identify it. If we're insecure about who we are, we push people away. Our lives are not like those color-coded file folders where love is in one yellow file, work is in the green file, kids are in the red file. The elements of our lives bleed together, and when we're unhappy in one area, it is going to have an impact on all other areas to varying degrees.

I didn't have any idea of what I was in for when I wanted to "fix" that one part of my life called marriage. I had no idea what I would discover about myself and what I would have to face in order to heal my brokenness. It required me to be brutally honest with myself, and it required a tenacity to never stop swimming the moat, no matter how tired I became. I could rest, but eventually I had to lift my head up and begin swimming again.

CHAPTER 3

Playing with Fire

God doesn't give you the people you want, He gives you the people you need. To help you, to hurt you, to leave you, to love you, and to make you the person you were meant to be.
—Unknown

Michael was a man in many ways and a boy in others. Michael was tall, broad-shouldered, very muscular, and devilishly handsome, with an amazing smile that lit up his dark eyes when he saw me. His confidence and charm commanded attention. He was well spoken, but not well traveled; he had simple tastes but big goals and dreams for himself. He was young, handsome, confident, charismatic, expressive, and affectionate.

Michael and I began spending time together and getting to know each other as friends toward the end of my marriage, and then during my separation. It didn't take long for us to establish a deep connection and for me to be on the receiving end of some simple but dangerous advances. Something as simple as a text message that read, "Good morning, Beautiful," sent me spiraling for the entire day. I had never once been called beautiful by anyone—ever. There is power in words, and those words were like oxygen to me at a time when I felt like I was on life support.

Once we acknowledged our attraction, the first two months with Michael were a whirlwind—both of us caught in this vortex of intense feelings and emotion and quickly falling for each other. He became an escape for me during this difficult period; a dangerous escape.

We spent a lot of time together and would talk for hours. Michael would wrap himself around me, holding me tightly, caressing me as we would lie on the couch together watching TV. His body would press against mine, and his enormous physical presence made me feel safe. He was open and expressive, wanting to talk about every aspect of life, love, family, sex, as if nothing were off-limits. He was spontaneous. He listened to me, made me feel important. He would take his time making love to me, being amazingly gentle and strong and passionate at the same time. He would look at me; he would see me. In thirty-eight years, that had never happened before. He relished parts of my body that I had been ashamed about my entire life, making me feel sensual and beautiful. Michael would drive to my apartment late at night just so he could lie next to me and wake up holding me. When we couldn't be together, he would call me at night so we could fall asleep together over the phone, listening to each other's breathing. He respected my mind and asked my opinion. He said he loved me.

> Playing with fire is a predictable activity.
> Not surprisingly, I got burned.

Playing with fire is a predictable activity. Not surprisingly, I got burned. Just as I became consumed by this drug, needing hit after hit, he began to pull away. What Michael was drawn to in me was my confidence. Interestingly enough, what he was attracted to was that distant, cold, all-knowing shell of a woman. But once I became vulnerable to him and fell in love with him, all that confidence and swagger went away. I became weak and vulnerable, insecure and desperate for his attention. In turn, he began making less and less time for me, making me feel very small and unimportant in his very big life. He would tell me he had plans but not share with me what they were or who they were with. There were times I ran into him in public and he would barely acknowledge my presence. The more I reached, the more he pulled away. Then friends would see him out spending time with other women. He later told me, "I love you, but I'm not in love with you," harsh words to hear. That was where the short, but intense, relationship ended.

As any good junkie would do, I became more and more desperate for the possibility that we might get back together and I could get just one more hit of that drug. I didn't sleep, I was barely eating, I lost a lot of weight; I couldn't concentrate at work and was forgetting basic things. I'm certain there were days that I shouldn't even have been driving, much less working and making million-dollar decisions at my job.

Michael had awakened feelings in me that I had never felt before, and I was terrified that without him, I would never feel that way again. I feared I would never feel that kind of love again, I would never be seen again, I would never be adored again, I would never feel safe or sexy or wanted again. It was as if I thought I would go back to being the same woman I was when I was married if he wasn't there.

But it wasn't about him. It never was. It was always about me.

This was about my own insecurities and fears that I had never confronted. I didn't really believe that I was beautiful. Maybe I was never worthy of affection. What if I was unlovable? Surely there was something lacking in me. I believed that I wasn't good enough. I wasn't smart enough, attractive enough, exciting enough. Those were some insecurities I had been carrying around for years but had never spoken, never given life. They haunted me and now they were all coming to the surface, demanding to be acknowledged.

My relationship with God evolved tremendously during this time. I attended church, sitting in the balcony so as to be a bit removed but being moved by the sermons that always seemed to speak directly to me. For the first time in my life, I was finally, actively seeking God's presence in my life. Because for the first time, I knew I needed His help, His grace, His presence. I couldn't do this on my own. I was hurting and didn't know how to make the pain go away. I was at a point where I felt that I had no other choice but to put my life in God's hands. I prayed every day. My prayer, more often than not, was *God, I can't do this. Please take away this pain.*

I shed more tears in that year after my marriage than I had in my entire life. Yes, I was the one who left. Yes, I was the one who allowed someone into my life and heart. But neither of those things absolved me from the pain that I would experience in the coming months and years.

Love Lesson in Truth

Breaking open my heart the way I did exposed me to more love, more emotion, more feeling, and more experiences, but also to more pain that I had ever felt before. I had never allowed anyone that far into my heart or my soul before, and exposing that raw nerve can be a risky endeavor. But even in risk, there's growth and beauty and truth, and I am grateful for it. I let someone know me and truly see me.

It doesn't matter if we're talking about fame, success, money, or love; the more we reach and grasp and struggle for something in a desperate, anxious way, the more that which we're seeking will elude us. We have to be able to put our energy and love out there and see what comes to us, rather than suffocating something or someone into doing what we want.

I learned something about myself that I didn't know before. The emotions I was feeling for the first time in my life—the feelings of being loved, seen, and adored—may have been brought to the surface by someone else, but those feelings were mine. And if they were mine, then I could feel them again.

I had to break wide open to really allow that wall to come down around me and begin facing my truths. Without that exposure to such profound sadness and pain, I'd probably still be hiding today. I began the process of allowing my insecurities—all the lies I told myself—to be exposed. And once they were in the light of day, I could begin to understand them as the wounds they were, nurture them a bit, and begin to heal. But the process of healing takes some time, and it can be an incredibly difficult part of the journey.

CHAPTER 4

Reflections of Brokenness

We don't get to stay in hiding until we are whole;
Jesus invites us to live as an inviting woman
now and find our healing along the way.
—John and Stasi Eldredge, *Captivating*

I was broken and numb following my breakup with Michael and after my divorce became final. There was both an emptiness and a permanence to this new life. There were no words to describe how my heart felt during this time. I would think about the life I had less than a year before—such a seemingly perfect, suburban, secure bubble of a life—that was now one of exposed feelings involving pain, insecurities, and truths I still couldn't fully own. I couldn't go back to the woman I was—the overly confident, controlling woman in the bubble—yet I didn't know who I was becoming. So I was stuck in this uncertain space in between, walking around ready to hand my heart over to virtually anyone willing or broken enough to take it.

Julian and I became close quickly, as was seeming to become a pattern. He was loving and affectionate, open and communicative, strong and confident, spiritual, with a strong faith in God, while still having times of discreet and absolute vulnerability. When we were together, we were consumed with each other, and when we were apart, we thought about each other incessantly. We said we loved each other. It felt real. He was a grown man, a mature man, a few years older than I. He had an extremely successful career, the million-dollar home, the art collection, the expensive cars, the seemingly picture-perfect, country-club life. That was his mask. He also had a wife who insulted, dehumanized, and emasculated him in front of his children, whom he fiercely loved. Mercifully for everyone, our relationship ended almost as quickly as it began.

There were other men who were not individually very important to me, but whose collective message was significant. Each of these men was in a relationship with another woman but would reach out to me, want to be with me. Somehow, I was always good enough to be the other woman, but never good enough to be the only woman for these men. Surely, that a handful of these men tried to enter my life at the same time can be no coincidence; the only common denominator was me.

A wise friend named Gabby once told me, "There are no coincidences—only God at work in your life." So why was I here? What was I supposed to learn? Where is the truth in this?

"There are no coincidences—only God at work in your life."

Although it's tempting to delve into the heart of a man who is serially unfaithful to the woman in his life, it's far more interesting (and certainly more productive) to attempt to discern why I continued to choose or attract this type of man and why I was making myself most open and available to those that had the potential to hurt me the most.

Some of the men I met during this time would send flirtatious text messages or e-mails but would not ask me out on a date. Three men also asked me for money. They might screw me or take money from me but had no particular interest in knowing me or loving me or caring for my heart. "What kind of man does that sort of thing?" you might ask. The kind of man I was allowing to continue to play a role in my life, because I hadn't yet shut it all down. When I responded to their messages, met them for drinks, or even gave them money, I was feeding the monster. I was using all these levers as bait to try to catch their hearts, because deep down I didn't believe that everything else I had to give was sufficient. I still had the false belief that I wasn't enough or that I wasn't worthy of real love.

It was during this time that my prayer, more often than not, was, "Lord, please just don't give up on me." Although I was still hurting, I somehow knew that this place I was in would not last forever. I knew there was a light on the other side beckoning me, and I knew there was a beautiful, bright light inside of me just dying to get out.

Love Lessons in Truth

The way you allow yourself to be treated by others is a reflection of your own self-worth. If I didn't think much of myself, then why should anyone else? My heart is my most precious gift from God, but I wasn't yet treating it as such. If I didn't treat my heart as the beautiful gift that it was, why should they? I allowed these men to treat me as if I were at their disposal—pulling me off the bench when it was convenient for them, because I didn't respect myself enough to demand otherwise. I kept naively believing that sex or money would lead to love and that someone would come along to save me from my own unhappiness. I was delusional enough to think that once I had a man's love, I would suddenly, magically learn to love myself.

It was impossible for me to hand over the responsibility of my own happiness to anyone else. No one could do that for me, and frankly, it was unfair for me to have asked that of them. Most of them could barely take care of themselves. I had to learn to love myself and accept myself for where I was. Loving all the parts—the good, the bad, the strong, the weak, the joyful, the needy, the fabulous diva, and the sinner—it all had to begin with me. And it had to include God, because this was something I clearly couldn't do on my own.

CHAPTER 5

You're off the Hook

I have to stop looking for a man to save
me, and just save myself.
—Sharon Pope

After a divorce or some similarly life-shaking, identity-changing event, we all have the potential to go through a destructive phase as we find our new selves. I've seen far too many women experience it to not discuss it within the context of this book. We're hurting and there are times when we're looking for something, someone, anything to make that pain go away, even if it's only for a short while. If you're like me, you started passing out your heart as if it were candy at Halloween, regardless of the mask that was staring you in the face.

For a long time, I was waiting for someone to come along and save me. Save me from whom? Myself? My own choices? My own destructive behavior? My own insecurities? I kept looking for someone who could see the princess deep down inside of me and have the strength and desire to pull it out into the light. I wanted so badly to have someone come into my life who would be "man enough" to make me forget about all the other men who came before and hurt me so badly. I wanted them to do for me what I couldn't do for myself at the time. Not surprisingly, I never found that.

I was seeking the impossible. No man could do that for me. I had to heal that brokenness myself. I had to do that work.

> No man could do that for me. I had to
> heal that brokenness myself.

To begin, I needed to acknowledge and take responsibility for what I had done, the hurt that I had caused to both myself and others. At the same time, I needed to be able to see the wounds that remained. That's the part where you see yourself as you really are. No more masks, no more lies, no more hiding. I had to be able to look my own truth in the eyes.

Many times, when we see the truth as it really is, we need to learn the power of forgiveness. Forgiveness, for me, was seeing myself through a softer lens and being able to love myself in spite of the mistakes. I had to find the courage to forgive myself, and I had to find the compassion to forgive those who hurt me. This is an important step to healing, and it is one on which many get stuck. Forgiveness doesn't mean that what happened was okay; it's just a simple acknowledgment that we're all on our own paths, trying to find our own truths, and trying to get better. We're going to make mistakes; we might even hurt others, and when we do, we accept responsibility. Unless we make the choice to forgive, we risk wallowing in that darkness and remaining imprisoned.

If those beliefs I held about myself weren't actually true, then what was the truth? What if I really was worthy of love? What would happen if I realized that I had a tremendous amount to give in a relationship? What if I let people know me and see me—even if everything they saw wasn't perfect? If I didn't have it all together, all the time, maybe that would be okay. Maybe I was beautiful. Maybe I could get back that laughter in my eyes and that joy in my smile. What would be possible if I began to believe that I was "enough"? I had to name all the lies I was carrying around and then replace those stories with what was true.

Love Lessons in Truth

Once I could see the lies that caused me pain, give them a little nurturing and love, I could see what was true and what was real in my life. The peace came to me once I began appreciating my own light and sat in the presence of its glow. I was able to hold my own heart and my newly healed wounds gently and just love them a little. If ever I struggled with that, I just tried to see myself through God's eyes. In doing so I began to understand the blessing these experiences were to my life. I saw how the lessons were making me stronger and wiser. The wounds that shook my foundation were the catalyst that ended up bringing about that person that was trying so hard to come out. The struggles along the way were what exposed my heart, made me vulnerable, and taught me self-love. The truth was ultimately what brought me to peace.

Socrates said, "This is a universe that does not favor the timid." Part of the process is our ability to get to the real, brutal, honest truth about ourselves—not what we hope the truth is or what we want the truth to be, but what it actually is. And when we can stare that truth in the eyes, then we can heal it.

Although we may have guides that help us along the way, this is something we have to do for ourselves. You're the only one who knows the directions to your version of happiness. We cannot look for someone else to provide us the map.

But here's the thing: we're worth that journey. We're worth the work. Our light is worth pulling out of the darkness. God didn't create any of us to be a hollow shell of a human being. Our true selves are worth finding.

Once we save ourselves and become our own knights in shining armor, we begin to find the peace we're seeking. Only then will we finally recognize it and be able to nurture it. Only then have we earned it.

CHAPTER 6

In Love with Possibility

> If you give your committed love to a person, an idea, or a cause, even should that person, idea, or cause be taken from you, or proven false, you will be a better lover—of anyone, of anything—for the experience.
> —Kate Braestrup, *Marriage and Other Acts of Charity*

I give my love in so many ways. If I believe in you, you have my encouragement. If you're helping others, and that cause touches me in some way, you have my heart. If you inspire me to build something bigger than myself, to grow something out of nothing, or to do something others have not, you have my desire. There have been men in my life that speak of the possibilities of what they will accomplish, what they will become. There have been men in my life that speak of our possibilities and our future together.

Once they give it life, I begin to see it. I see it for them. I see it for us. I build on it and see it bigger than they had ever imagined. I genuinely believe in people. I see excellence in people. I see what people are capable of, even more than what they see for themselves. Personally, professionally, in their relationships, in love, I see how it could be …

… while ignoring how it actually is.

When I was dating, I could quickly and easily see the kind of relationship we could have—not the one we did have. I got caught up in the idea of what we could be together: unstoppable, happy, committed. I believe that if asked, some of these men would tell you that they were better people when we were together, because they had someone who believed in them.

The time when he is attempting to win my affection—talking about all his hopes and dreams and of what he hopes to accomplish in this life—that's him at his best. It will never get better than when he's trying to win love and attention. That's him at his most hopeful, his biggest and brightest.

I tried to make the moment I had with such men more than what it was because at my core I'm a relationship girl. I tried to create conversation and connection where there was none, confidence where it was lacking, and faith in the future when they couldn't see more than fifteen minutes in front of themselves. But you cannot create what does not exist. You cannot bring about in a man what does not live at his core. He's not holding out on you ... it's simply not there. And what he lacks is not an inadequacy in you. But we like to take it on as our own sometimes: if I were only stronger, prettier, more confident, more successful, more loving ... then it would have worked.

What he lacks is not an inadequacy in you.

So many women fall down that path of thinking that they're strong enough to change a man; I most certainly did. I was strong, passionate, and giving enough to equip a man with whatever he needed to become the man I thought I saw inside of him. The reality was that all of my strength, all of my passion, and all of the generosity I had in me couldn't make these men whole, couldn't make them driven, couldn't make them successful, couldn't even make them strong, committed, honest, or loving. That's something they had to do for themselves. That's their journey.

They missed the point, but so did I.

Sharon Pope

Love Lessons in Truth

I should have believed Maya Angelou when she said, "When someone shows you who they are, believe them." I was busy creating the fairy tale in my head, rather than living in the reality of the moment. While I was dreaming of what could be, he was thinking about what is. While I was focused on the possibilities, he didn't see beyond the reality in front of him, thinking about this one day, this one date, this one night.

We can't fall in love with the man he could be. We can't fall in love with the potential we see. If we fall in love with a man, we need to love the man who's standing there in front of us. That's his most authentic self. Take a man at face value. He's not holding back; he's showing us who he is.

I can *help* any man achieve his greatest heights as a human being, but I cannot do it for him. I can be tremendously supportive and incredibly helpful. I can be there to love him through his failures and cheer him on through his victories. I can be the quiet strength and the silent partner, letting him know that he is enough. But, I cannot create or carry a dream for someone else. I cannot expect someone to change for my benefit or even their own.

It's quite enough most days to stay present in our own lives and make the strides and changes we each need, without attempting to do that for someone else.

CHAPTER 7

My Heart

You love me like a champion.
—Ledisi, "Stay Together"

Derrick and I met through an online dating website. I had been dating through those sites for a while and had become pretty jaded as a result of some of the experiences. So even though Derrick was disarmingly attractive, my expectations weren't high.

I knew that I still had some wounds to heal, so I wasn't dating much, and that was fine. I had earned a break from the madness. I was reading a lot, journaling almost every day, and my growth was slow but steady.

Even before we met in person, I knew Derrick was different. He asked questions that told me that he wanted to get beyond the superficial woman's profile on the website. He actually wanted to take me out on a date, sit across from me, have a meal together, and get to know each other (what a concept!). Even though he had hundreds of e-mails within a day or so of posting his profile online, for whatever reason he said that my e-mail stood out to him, because it was the only one he responded to. I can't even recall what I said, but it was clearly full of wit and magic! In one of our introductory e-mails, he said he was "captivated by me." The title of the book by John and Stasi Eldredge that literally changed my life is *Captivating* (quoted in this book). Interesting choice of words; I was intrigued.

He lived approximately an hour away, and he drove into the city to meet me for sushi. As we were walking to the restaurant, he took me by surprise by walking on the outside of me, closest to the street. He opened the door for me and held out my chair before I sat down. No one had ever done that before. He was sweet and kind, secure and confident. He was a firefighter and paramedic and loved what he did for a living; I could tell that he was genuinely good at it. He had been married previously for eighteen years, had two children, and had dated only one other woman since his divorce. Ours was the very first date he had been on since posting his picture on the online dating site. I told him that although he didn't know it yet, he had just won the lottery by meeting me for his first Internet date (after all, I had to kiss a lot of frogs before meeting him). This one was different.

I honestly didn't know what to do with him, because I didn't trust myself with a heart that pure. I didn't trust myself, my own instincts, or my ability to love again. My fear was that I would ultimately end up breaking his heart too, just as I had done with my ex-husband, and he didn't deserve that; so in my mind I extended that to mean he must deserve someone better than me. Clearly, it was I who was still too wounded to have a real relationship and let someone into my heart again. At least, not yet. But we always had a great time together, having real, honest conversations with each other. I began to trust him. I also had a strong belief that God was at work.

Derrick hung in there with me—believing for more. He saw a heart in me that I had lost track of a while ago. He saw a future that I couldn't because I was still living in fear. I believe he saw the woman I was trying to become.

It was during this time that I would pray, *Lord, please help me to be worthy of Derrick's love.*

I would love to tell you that there was one night that God spoke to me, and it was vivid and memorable and meaningful, with lots of lights and fireworks. That would make for such a great story. But when God's actively at work in my life, it's much more like a flowing river that permeates my thoughts and stills my spirit, and I float along holding onto His loving hand. It wasn't that long before I was able to see Derrick through somewhat new eyes and a healed heart, and I began to let him "see" me. I opened up. I began to see our future. I stopped being so scared.

When God's actively at work in my life, it's much more like a flowing river that permeates my thoughts and stills my spirit, and I float along holding onto His loving hand.

Derrick and I moved in together, furthering our relationship and melting into each other's lives. This became a different kind of love for me, one that I had not yet known. It wasn't that quick, intense, heartbreaking kind of love. This was a slow, graceful, easy, and trusting kind of love. He was and is passionate and confident, gentle and soulful. He held me tightly; we always fell asleep and awoke in each other's arms. He would come up behind me and wrap his arms around me and kiss my neck. He kisses me while holding the back of my neck or with both hands holding my face. He still walks closest to the street, grasping my hand a little more firmly, and steps out in front of me as we cross a street. He pulls out chairs, opens car doors, and tells me I'm beautiful or stunning every single day.

Once he told me that he actively looks for ways to make my life easier. For someone who had always done the heavy lifting in every relationship, it's really nice to feel that someone's taking care of you. He knew that my grandmother's hope chest was an important heirloom for me, as my grandmother had passed several years prior, and this was one of my only items from her home. It badly needed refinishing, and I had never done such a thing before and didn't know where to start. Derrick had that chest completely refinished when I came home from work one day. It was a beautiful gesture.

Derrick met my parents early in our relationship and they liked him right away. One time, my father was in a nursing home for a few weeks while he recovered from back surgery, and Derrick and I went to visit him. My dad wasn't feeling like himself, because he hadn't shaved in days. He was unable to get up and stand long enough to shave himself, so Derrick shaved my father. He used a hot, wet towel and gently wrapped it around my father's face to soften the skin and hairs. He then lathered up shaving cream on his face and slowly, gently, confidently shaved my dad. I swear to you, it was one of the sweetest things I had ever seen someone do for another human being—and this was my love, my heart, doing this for my father.

Derrick and I lived together in an apartment painfully small for two people and an eighty-pound dog. It was only about nine hundred square feet, but we made it work there for a little over a year. I had someone tell me, "It must be love if you two can live together in that small of a space for that long without killing each other." We had come to love downtown living and wanted to buy a condo where we could walk to different places. We found something that we both fell in love with and could be ours. "Ours" is very different than a place that was mine that he moved into or vice versa. "Ours" meant it was something we chose together and could create together. "Ours" meant there was a commitment and a future that now we both could see.

Derrick settles me, he settles my heart. He is equal and perfect parts of peace and passion. If I'm ever anxious, he's my rock; if I'm ever apprehensive, he inspires me and gives me confidence; when I need love, he's my champion. When I'm with him, I am never fearful; I know that I am protected. His faith in God is enormous, never-ending, and inspiring. He doesn't preach at you or try to force his beliefs on you; he just has that quiet confidence about God at work in his life. He's strong: physically, mentally, and spiritually.

Last year, on New Year's Eve, on the beaches of St. Lucia, I married my heart, my love, my champion.

Love Lessons in Truth

Learn to trust that God is at work when it comes to matters of the heart. Learn to trust His timing. Work on becoming the healthiest soul you know how to be so that when love presents itself, you'll be ready (or, like me, at least a little closer to being ready). He knows you. He knows your heart. He knows your prayers, both spoken and silent, so He knows what you want. More importantly, He knows what you need.

Derrick makes me—allows me, draws out in me—the very best version of myself. With him I am totally at ease in my own skin and with my own heart. I have peace. I used to talk about finding that "big love," the kind of love that envelops you, consumes you, carries you. With Derrick I know a love that's bigger than I ever could have imagined, greater than I ever even knew how to pray for, larger than I ever knew existed.

CHAPTER 8

Affection and Connection

If we are not careful, we will lose the ability to see such things as beauty, truth, or even affection. More importantly, you may close your eyes to what your soul needs you most to see.
—Erwin Raphael McManus, *Soul Cravings*

Many studies have proven all the benefits people receive through a simple touch. It's been proven to play an important role in people's physical and emotional health. It has been shown to help reduce stress, decrease pain, and increase our ability to cope, and it most certainly has a tremendous impact on our interpersonal relationships. There is touch therapy to help children with severe autism speak; physical therapists rely on touch to help guide their patients and retrain their muscles; massage therapy releases tired, tight muscles. The human touch can help a child grow up healthy, happy, and well adjusted; it can also help an elderly patient in a nursing home keep from becoming restless and agitated.

I've mentioned that my first husband and I did not have a terribly intimate relationship. I'm not talking about sex; I'm talking about a lack of nonsexual intimate physical contact and an emotional closeness. When we met, that was fine; we were getting to know each other, and not a great deal of touching seemed completely appropriate.

I honestly didn't know any different. I grew up with a family that didn't hug very often and didn't tell one another, "I love you." I rarely saw my parents hold hands or kiss. My grandparents demonstrated the same behavior. We simply weren't affectionate toward one another as a family. Don't get me wrong; just because my family didn't express or demonstrate it doesn't mean they didn't love one another. They did, deeply, and I always knew that. The "touch" in our household was more often than not my brother and me beating up each other, and my poor mother trying to pull us apart. So when I met and later married Jason, I didn't know that anything was wrong with how we interacted; that's all I had ever known or experienced. As a matter of fact, for most of my young adult life, it made me uncomfortable to see or experience any public displays of affection, because it was so foreign to me.

Looking back on my first marriage, however, I realize that the lack of touching was the source from which many of our problems sprang. We didn't know how to truly connect to each other emotionally, psychologically, or physically, because we didn't have a closeness with each other. Let me repeat that, because it's important: *my husband and I didn't have a closeness with each other.* In a marriage—any marriage—there will be times when it will feel like it's just the two of you against the world, and if you don't know the soul that is standing beside you, all you feel during those times is alone. You feel the weight of carrying that load—whatever troubles come your way—all squarely on your shoulders. I didn't know the heart and soul that was standing beside me. I didn't know if he could help me weather a storm or take care of me or make me feel loved and secure in times of trouble. He probably didn't know the same about the person standing beside him either. So there we were—each of us alone—but next to each other.

If you don't know the soul that is standing beside you, all you feel during those times is alone.

The only time my first husband and I would touch was when we had sex. Sex, I knew, was a requirement in a marriage—everyone said so. I didn't know it was something we were supposed to or were allowed to enjoy (thank you very much,

Catholic upbringing, for that one). I didn't realize it was a way to connect on a deeper level with your partner. I just knew it was "part of the deal." Let's just say, I didn't know what I didn't know.

Over time my first husband and I both came to know that every touch somehow led to sex. That was the only time we showed affection. If one of us wasn't interested in sex at that particular moment (say, while I was folding laundry), then the touch was unwelcomed. And whenever you're on the receiving end of your partner declining your sexual advances, it doesn't exactly give you the confidence to step up to the plate over and over again. So over time he didn't step up as often. We didn't know how to touch each other, how to connect with each other or just let the other person feel love and support. So, for us, that emotional distance became amplified over time.

Love Lessons in Truth

Touch is now profoundly important to me. Closeness is an absolute necessity. Intimacy—knowing someone's heart and soul—is a blessing. These aren't things you put in your online dating profile by the way, like blonde hair and blue eyes. It requires a connection between two people that either exists or doesn't. You cannot be forced to trust someone with your heart, and you cannot be coerced into sharing your soul. Allowing someone to know you and touch you requires a certain degree of vulnerability on your part, as you may be allowing them to touch parts of you that you're not even particularly comfortable with yet.

Some nights with Derrick, we will lie together on the couch watching a movie. I will be lying against his chest, and he will have one hand wrapped around me and the other will be running his fingers through my hair. This calms me and makes me feel secure, but it relaxes him as well. We're that couple that's always sitting closely, holding hands, sneaking kisses. There's beauty and power in touch because it calms both the person giving and the person receiving the gift. That simple, selfless act creates a connection for us that is our deepest form of communication. Connection is like magic: you don't know exactly how it happens, but when it works, you stand there in awe of the feeling.

It is so clear to me that we need one another in this world. We were not created to be in isolation from one another. People cannot thrive without human contact. Relationships cannot grow deeper without the gift of closeness, touch, and intimacy. I need to know the soul of who stands beside me in this life. I need touch the way I need air, food, and water.

CHAPTER 9

Expectations

And if, by chance, we find each other, it's beautiful.
—Excerpt from The Gestalt Prayer, Friedrich (Fritz) Perls

In our lives and in our loves, we have expectations for ourselves, but mostly, when we're being honest, we have expectations for others. I used to say that I wanted a "good man," but apparently I needed to be a bit more articulate regarding the specifics before letting someone into my life, much less my heart (honest, faithful, unmarried, intelligent, etc.). I spent a great deal of time trying to change the men I was seeing into what I needed them to be for me. You'll notice that my expectations weren't for someone who was fluent in five languages or knew how to cook; changing a dishonest man into one that is honest is a tall order, but I never shy away from a challenge.

For that and so many other reasons, I think it's safe to say that when I began dating after my divorce, I hadn't a clue what I was doing. I became whatever I thought the "flavor of the month" wanted me to be. I knew my heart was genuine, but unfortunately I didn't know who I was, so I became whatever I needed to be in order for you to love me. You want me to be funny, I'll be funny. You want me to be smart and driven, I can do that. You want me to be sexy and sultry—well, I'll try. I was so preoccupied with trying to get you to fall in love with me that I lost myself in the process.

By the grace of God, I was seeing an extremely wise and helpful counselor, who helped me through this time in my life. It was during one particular session with him that I came to realize the truth about dating and trying to find someone special with whom I could share my heart. There is a delicate balance we play in trying to find the kind of person that we feel we deserve and trying to create the kind of person we feel we deserve. It requires us to be confident enough not only to be ourselves but also to give them space and freedom, allowing them to be themselves.

> It was not my place to set expectations for another human being. That's just another form of control.

It was not my place to set expectations for another human being. That's just another form of control. If someone bends to my expectations, then he won't be authentic when he is with me—essentially he will be living a lie that cannot be sustained. Eventually his true self will show, and I'll think I was duped: *This isn't the same man I thought he was* or *He changed!* In reality, all he did was become his authentic self. I needed to know who he really was in order for it to be real and in order for the relationship to stand a chance.

Likewise, I cannot live a lie. What good does it do to mislead someone into a relationship by becoming the person they want me to be rather than the person that I really am? That's not sustainable either. Eventually, the truth always comes out.

Love Lessons in Truth

Let him see you; let him know you. Let him experience the good and the bad, the strong and the weak parts. I know it sounds scary to take the mask off, but if we can love all the messy parts that make up the fabulous women that we are, then there's someone else out there that will too. Experience others as your authentic self, and you'll experience a power and freedom you may have never known.

For a relationship to work, it needs to be real for both hearts. Here's the good news: we no longer have to waste all that energy pulling on those many layers of trying to be someone we're not in order to please someone else. And they won't have to do it either. Those layers are just a mask of our true selves, and, by the way, those layers are a lot of work. They feel heavy and burdensome.

As we learn more about ourselves along this journey, we will inevitably become better people and better partners. Once I knew better and saw my authentic self more clearly, it was no longer enough to just have a "good man." I wanted a man that was worthy of my love. This didn't mean that I had it all figured out; I just became more comfortable and confident in my own skin and with my own contributions to a relationship. I came to know and love the precious gift of my heart, and so I stopped giving it away so easily.

As soon as I owned the fact that I wasn't always strong, that same self-awareness made me stronger. As soon as I admitted that I don't have all the answers, I received all the clarity I needed. As soon as I began to value the love I had to give, I stopped giving it so freely.

It comes back to living authentically. We all need to be who we are and allow others to be who they are at the core. Enough pretending, enough playing. If we find that a particular relationship is not what we want, then we can simply stop trying to force fit a relationship just because it happens to be the one staring us down at this particular moment. We can just simply stop. There will be others. When this one isn't right, there will be others. There will be as many as we need, until the one comes along where the blinders are lifted and the layers come off effortlessly. Let him do his thing, and you do yours. Embrace and celebrate who you are. Be curious about who he is. But don't force it. If it doesn't work for either or both of you, release the relationship and your expectations, and never look back.

CHAPTER 10

It's Always about Us

Broken finds broken; health finds health.
—Amy Bixel

I have a friend, Kerri, who I think is amazing; she is one of the best people I know, and I have so much love for her. She is smart, driven, talented, beautiful, generous, and funny. She is charming, witty, and the person that everyone adores. She loves her family, has a strong faith, is genuinely interested in others, and works hard. But, for the life of me, I could not figure out why she didn't see her worth. For more than a decade she had been with a man who had lied to her, stolen from her, run up her credit cards, become addicted to drugs, and very likely cheated on her. I didn't understand the attraction and why she stayed with him for as long as she did. She could have had any man she wanted, so why this one?

I have another friend, Stefanie, who has dated a man for years who has been controlling, distant, and unloving toward her. He has consistently made her feel as though she doesn't matter, that she is unimportant, simply reinforcing some of her own feelings of low self-worth. He doesn't trust people and, as a result, leads a very closed and secluded life. Yet she is fun and has many friends and an active life. She likes to travel and go out to eat at great restaurants, and loves a well-made cosmopolitan. She is pretty, smart as a whip, and talented. What is the attraction to this man?

I have a friend, Susan, whose husband tells her that he drinks too much because she's fat. Now, I could have a field day with that one! But the insights there are far too obvious. That is abusive and hateful and yet, she stays.

Women not recognizing their worth in this world has to be reaching epidemic proportions.

I looked at my own past relationships. It didn't matter which one: it could be the one who was so disconnected from his own feelings that he was emotionally dead. It could be the one whom I treated like gold and allowed him to walk all over me, time and again. It could be one who kept coming around with no idea how to connect with a woman. Or it could be the man who was so broken in his home life that he desperately sought love and acceptance in other places and with other people.

Here's a universal truth that nobody tells you, one that is not for some people, some of the time. It is one of the few truths I've found that is true for all types of people, all the time. No emotionally healthy person is attracted to and stays in a relationship with a broken person for any real length of time ... ever. Broken people find broken people, while healthy people find healthy people. No one that is secure in who they are, about what they deserve, and is emotionally available is ever really in a committed relationship with someone who is sad, broken, insecure, or feels undeserving of such love. It doesn't matter if it's me, you, my clients, my friends, or your friends. It doesn't happen.

I've seen couples who have tried to make that work. Kelly and Chris had been dating for a few years. Chris was an emotionally mature individual, but it was apparent that Kelly still had a lot a demons with which to contend. There was one evening when several of us all met at a local, upscale bar downtown for some cocktails. Once Kelly had a few too many drinks, she began flirting with many other people in the place, hanging on them, smiling, stopping just short of stealing a kiss. I was embarrassed for both Kelly and Chris. Kelly was inflicting a level of emotional abuse on Chris, and eventually that relationship ended. An emotionally healthy person simply won't stay in an abusive relationship, regardless of how much they love the person.

Another acquaintance, Austin, grew up in a home with a physically and emotionally abusive father. He shared only the briefest of details with me about the pain that was inflicted on his mother, and the understandable resentment he carries to this day for his father. But what he fails to see is that abuse comes in many forms. He has never, to my knowledge, put his hands on a woman. However, he thinks nothing of abusing women's hearts, as if it were some sick game. He tells them half-truths; he keeps women who genuinely care for him believing they're the only one, while he shares his life with many other women. Austin abuses women not physically, but emotionally. He would take great offense if someone told him he's perpetuating his own father's behavior. It's no coincidence that the only women he finds and attracts are broken.

No one deserves to be abused by another human being. Abuse begins from a broken place. For any human being to actively, intentionally hurt another means they're emotionally hurting themselves. However, allowing ourselves to be continually mistreated is our brokenness.

> …allowing ourselves to be continually
> mistreated is our brokenness.

Love Lessons in Truth

When we allow someone who's emotionally unhealthy or abusive into our lives, that just means our "man-picker" is broken—God knows mine was on the fritz for years. But to stay with someone who treats us as "less than" exposes the degree of our own brokenness.

It's always about us.

I couldn't maintain a whole, healthy relationship until I got emotionally healthy myself. I know that now. But at the time, I couldn't understand why even though I was a good person and had so much love to give to another, I kept finding men that hurt me. Even though I was honest and faithful, they were not. Being a good person didn't have anything to do with it. I didn't know who I was, what I wanted, or, better yet, what I needed and deserved. Before I could let someone else know me, I first had to know and be comfortable with myself. Before I would allow someone else to love me, I had to love myself. I did not get what I deserved until I knew how much more I really did deserve.

There are many articles written about the reasons we stay in bad relationships. Most of them focus on our own laziness in staying with the familiar, our fear of being alone, our lack of self-esteem or our belief that we'll never find another. Notice that all of those begin with the word "our." This is our stuff to heal. These are our truths. This is about our brokenness. This is our journey. And if we are going to stay in a relationship where we're not celebrated or respected, then we need to identify and own the reasons why, so that we can become healthier. The healthier we become emotionally, and the more compassion we have for ourselves on our journeys, the more we are able to make wise decisions that lead to loving, committed, real relationships that don't hurt.

CHAPTER 11

The Test

I am, indeed, a king, because I know how to rule myself.
—Pietro Aretino

The men I have loved and who have loved me almost always seem to come back at some point. My experience is that they won't when I'm grasping and reaching for them or mourning the hole they left in my heart. No, they did when I was at my most unsuspecting, long after I've gotten over the heartbreak, regained my strength, confidence and self-worth, potentially moved on to a new love, and was well into the healing phase. Somehow, that's when they tended to reappear.

Maybe it was my wholeness that they found attractive, that self-confidence that attracted me to them originally. Possibly they had some form of setback that made them recognize what they lost. Maybe they were looking for an ego boost, so they would know they've still "got it." Their reasons for coming back were really inconsequential.

When we're brutally honest with ourselves, there may still be some small, hidden part of us that's still hanging onto the hope of a reconciliation after a breakup, and such men know that. They know if that door is still ajar, even if only slightly, they will be able to test us to see if we will allow them to walk through it again.

Make no mistake; this is a test. When an old love comes back—particularly one that hurt us—we are being tested. Our response to this act will tell volumes about us, as well as our current state of mind.

Today, when the primary form of communication is through text messages, it is easy for someone to reach out through a text to see if there's still a stream of sunlight coming through that door crack, and therefore any hope of entering our world again. A simple "How have you been?" that comes in the form of a text or Facebook message may be harmless from anyone else, but from an ex-lover it is an invitation to disaster.

I've seen this play out so many times both in my own life and in the lives of my closest friends. It starts with harmless small talk: "How are you? What's new? Hope you're well." Then it moves to mild flirtation: "I love your new haircut. You look great. Lunch?" The moment we begin responding, the dialogue and accompanying mind games begin all over again. It escalates from small talk to mild flirtation, while we continue to tell ourselves the lie that it doesn't mean anything and we're in control of the conversation. We may be in control of the conversation, but we're playing a temptation game that is fraught with landmines and consequences. All of a sudden, he's on our mind more, at least more than he was a few weeks ago when we weren't thinking about him at all. He continues testing, all the while, never making himself vulnerable to us in any meaningful way.

> There's a slight redemptive victory in his coming back, even if only in some small way. It feeds our ego, so we allow it.

But we allow this. The second we respond, we open that cracked door just a little more and then a little more until the door is open wide enough for him to walk right through. We think we're in control and that we would never get back together with him, but we have to admit that he's pressing all of our ego buttons. There's a slight redemptive victory in his coming back, even if only in some small way. It feeds our ego, so we allow it. There's still that part of us that craves that attention from someone who took up residence in our heart so long ago, only to walk away. By allowing the conversation to continue, we're risking our hearts and disrespecting ourselves in the process.

This, by the way, is not limited to men coming back to women. I've seen women do this as well. Reading this, you may even see some of yourself in this story. I have a close friend who we'll call Gus who was married to his first wife for more than fifteen years. His wife cheated on him numerous times, ultimately asking him to leave and filing for divorce. They separated, he moved out and once the divorce was final, guess who came back? Yes, she did. She said she had realized her mistake and wanted him back, wanted to work it out, wanted to be able to (and I quote) have her cake and eat it too. She pursued this for nearly a year, all while her new boyfriend was living in her home with the two children from her marriage.

Here's the difference: Gus never opened that door. He didn't play games. It didn't matter how long she asked or pleaded, to his credit, he never gave her false hope that a reconciliation was a possibility. It wasn't. He approached that situation from a place of strength, and it says a great deal about his values, his self-worth, and his state of mind. For him, that door was closed and locked.

Love Lessons in Truth

When the most recent test occurred in my own life and my response was, "I'm not going to disrespect my partner that way," it stopped. The communications and flirtations from that person stopped and have never restarted. It was empowering. The power to continue the conversation and testing, as well as the power to shut it all down, lies within us.

The one truth, regardless of the person on the receiving end of the advances, is that when this happens our response (or lack thereof) has a whole lot more to do with us than it does them.

CHAPTER 12

Vulnerability Is Not a Four-Letter Word (But Control Should Be!)

> We're afraid to be vulnerable. We're afraid to be soft. We're afraid to be hurt ... So we become controlling and aggressive and vicious.
> —Iyanla Vanzant

You know this woman; it is likely either you or someone close to you. I lived most of my early adult life as this woman. This woman tries to control the people and circumstances around her. She thinks that taking charge of every aspect of her life will somehow lessen the fears or anxieties, maybe even dull the pain. We pretend that we're in complete control of what age we will be when we marry and at what age we will have our first child. We find ourselves reaching for control at work, trying to prove our worthiness among our peers; we attempt to control our children, at times not allowing them the opportunity to fail or find their own way in life; among our friends, we try to be the planner, the one never left out of the action, the center of attention. We try to control people's reactions, opinions, and perceptions of us by donning our daily mask.

But where it is most obvious, and most damaging, is in our relationships with the ones closest to us, those we love the most. I have seen women who absolutely dominate their men as if they're trying to train a dog. They belittle him, speaking with sarcasm and leading him around, guiding and directing his life for him, telling him where to turn left, how to chew his food, what to say, as if he is unable to move through life on his own.

I've seen this woman. I used to look at her in the mirror every day, prior to my transformation. I was married at the time, and there was virtually no decision in that household that didn't have my stamp of approval on it. There were no plans with friends that I had not made. There was never a meal served that I had not thought of or prepared. I decided when we would have sex. I decided what movies we would see and when and where we would vacation.

As a result of my controlling, I became tired, tired of always having to be "on." Tired of working all day and then coming home and still being "on the job," making the decisions, making dinner, taking care of the home. I never felt taken care of, because I didn't allow it. After all, "I've got this," remember? I pushed him away, because I didn't want to admit that I needed or wanted anyone's help. And then I became resentful that no one was taking care of me.

Even after my divorce, when I began dating again, I tried to create the love I was seeking. I foolishly tried to mold a man (that is, control a man) into what I thought I needed him to be for me, rather than taking him at face value for who he was showing me he was in his heart and soul.

Nothing good can come from trying to control someone else. Women were not meant to be controlling. For that matter, human beings are not meant to attempt to control one another. Looking back in history, any time one population has attempted to control another, bad things happened. We need look no further than the days when slavery was condoned to know that this is not God's will for us. As a matter of fact, our Creator Himself chose to not try to control us, by giving each of us free will. If He can let that go and leave us to our own devices, maybe there's hope for us controlling women after all.

There was even an article written by Tara Kelly in The Huffington Post, entitled, *Dominant Women Have Less Sex, Study Says.* It referenced a study by Johns Hopkins that found that dominant and assertive women had one hundred times less sex, and the more household decisions they made (as opposed to joint decisions), the less intimacy they had with their partners.

It's tragic, really. We control because we fear and despise that feeling of vulnerability. We think we're somehow safe if we never show ourselves or make ourselves vulnerable to another human being. We think we will never be hurt if we never actually place ourselves in the position of being wounded. But likewise, we'll never be truly seen, or known, or loved.

> We control because we fear and despise that feeling of vulnerability.

Women have some unique challenges in the workplace today as it relates to the topics of control and vulnerability, because to a certain degree, they're opposing forces. One is what you think, and the other is what you feel. One is a learned behavior, while the other is intrinsic.

Unfortunately, today the majority of people in leadership roles in business believe that there is no place for vulnerability in corporate America. (I happen to profoundly disagree with this, but that's an entirely different topic. See Brené Brown's 2012 TED Talk, *Listening to Shame*: http://www.youtube.com/watch?v=L0ifUM1DYKgIf.) Showing vulnerability at work, particularly as a manager, is widely thought to be the same thing as showing fear and insecurity. You cannot lead others where they want to go if you cannot instill confidence that you know where you're going and how to get there. That's what so many leadership courses will teach you (and deodorant commercials too, by the way: "Never let them see you sweat."). So at work women are expected, encouraged, and rewarded when we're in control, when we've got the answers, and when we've got our team marching in lockstep with us. That's the world that a successful businesswoman operates within most days.

Unfortunately, that trait has bled over into our personal relationships. We're supposed to somehow play the strong and controlling leader at work and then magically turn it off and become a completely different person when we walk through the front door at home. And now that we're essentially connected 24/7 through technology, how can we compartmentalize the controlling woman we're encouraged to be at work and the vulnerable woman we're supposed to be at home? Talk about living with a mask!

We're "allowed" to be vulnerable at home, with our life partner, right? If not with them, then who? The answer to that question is frightening. Because if we're not going to open ourselves up to being vulnerable to the people we love, we likely will not allow that God-given vulnerable side to show, to anyone, ever; or we allow it, but it's with someone outside our marriage that we can see through a different lens. One scenario is sad, the other dangerous; both are frightening and have some dire consequences.

Love Lessons in Truth

I believe that when women are controlling in their relationships with men, it comes with some catastrophic results. The man we love may lose, or possibly never really find, his self-esteem within our relationship because he didn't have a partner that believed in him. That means that he will never grow into the role of caretaker and provider for the family, the role he was created to play and the role that brings him a sense of pride. Disrespect within any relationship is like a cancer that, if untreated, will consume and destroy that which is in its path. And, along the way, through all of our controlling, we may lose respect for the one we pledged to love "until death do you part."

Upon this learning in my life, I not only stopped fighting it for myself, I stopped seeking out men who wanted it, needed it, or looked for that in a woman (there are some men who expect to be told what to do by their partner). I became all too familiar with her and simply decided that I didn't want to be her any longer. I wanted to be taken care of. I wanted to know that arrangements were made, things were fixed, bills were paid, dinner was arranged and obligations were met. I wanted a confident man who would step up to the plate without fear of striking out. I wanted him to feel comfortable with me knowing that I'm down for him no matter what, knowing that I'm on his side, cheering him on each day. In doing so, he becomes the man he is meant to be. He has the opportunity to provide for me and that helps him live his own natural, strong, confident, authentic life. It also helps me to become the confident, successful and secure woman I am meant to be.

Women were made to be vulnerable—not mousy, certainly not weak—but at ease, at peace; graceful, with an open heart, giving and caring. There's got to be a reason why we are the ones with the ability to bring life into the world and to mother and nurture children. Vulnerability doesn't lessen who we are or our voice, it enhances it. We all need to just stop fighting it. I fear we may have gone too far on our pendulum of independence. We need to let go of that control and allow ourselves to feel, to open our hearts and to become vulnerable to another. We can allow ourselves to be cared for and respected simultaneously. We can give someone else the gift of being the provider for the family and still earn a high income—it's a state of mind based on how we view our roles in the relationship. We don't need to hold back and we shouldn't pretend like we're the puppet master. We need to let life come to us a bit without knowing exactly what that looks like.

Put your heart and mind at rest when it comes to your partner; he may surprise you, knowing he's got you in his corner. He may just become the best version of himself; and you, yours.

CHAPTER 13

Honor and Cherish

With all that I am, and all that I have, I honor you.
—Service of Christian marriage

While the words *honor* and *cherish* are common in almost every wedding ceremony, they are not words we use each day with each other. As my own wedding draws near, I've given more thought to these words, what they mean and how to make them real in my life and in the life of our upcoming marriage.

When I think of showing someone honor in the context of marriage, I think it's showing them what a privilege it is to be married to them. It should be a privilege to be The One in his heart, in his life, in his soul. That's sacred ground and should be revered. I should be proud to hold that place in his life and proud to be witness to his life.

That definition might provide some guidance as to how I think about honoring Derrick and honoring our life together. Placing him and his heart on the proverbial pedestal means doing things for him just to make his life easier or more enjoyable. It's intentionally doing loving, selfless acts so that he not only hears that I love him but also feels it. It also means that even when he's not beside me, I will behave as if he is; disrespect often occurs when the person that's significant isn't present. It means encouraging him throughout his journey and helping him become the best version of himself.

The word *cherish*, as stated in *Webster's Dictionary*, means "to hold dear, to treat with affection and tenderness." The word draws for me a visual of a very small hand resting in the palm of a very large hand. It's holding something or someone with great care, not grasping with a closed hand, just gently supporting.

To cherish someone in marriage is to know them and to know their heart. It feels good to be in a relationship where you can know someone and really see them, but it is also a wonderful feeling to be known, to be seen, and to know that you live in the warmth of another's heart. By living out the vow to cherish, we are committing to treating that person with love, affection, care, and tenderness for a lifetime.

> To cherish someone in marriage is also to know them and to know their heart.

Why can't we use those words more often? Why can't we use them outside of marriage vows? I want to be in a relationship with my family and friends where we can honor and cherish one another, through open hearts of listening and acceptance (even when we don't agree). I want to learn how to extend that kind of love to people I meet, people I care about, people I hold dear—maybe even people I don't know or people I fear. Those words can transform relationships, if we let them.

The vows we take in marriage don't ask us to state how we feel about that person, right then, in that moment. On the day of our wedding is when we see this person through a lens where they can do no wrong and we think we will always feel the way we do in that particular moment when we say "I will." But that moment changes, the relationship changes, it goes through transformations, just as we do. It ebbs and flows just like the ocean, and although it might threaten to pull you under, sometimes you'll just need to float on the surface of the water and enjoy the ride. To say that we will honor and cherish this person is intentional. It's saying that even when this particular euphoric feeling passes, we will be deliberate about the way we love each other, deliberate about the way we respect each other. We won't just go through the motions. We will be proud to stand beside that person, renewing our commitment to honor and cherish the miraculous gift of love each and every day.

Love Lessons in Truth

This I can tell you: once you give your heart and soul to someone who deserves it, sees it, respects it, and nurtures it, everything changes. We become open to possibility, we love more deeply, we believe for more. Our faith expands, making room for us, for him and for the enormous love of our Creator. It feels good, it feels right, it feels healthy. It feels like home.

CHAPTER 14

Love

A strong woman
is one who feels deeply
and loves fiercely.
Her tears flow
Just as abundantly as her laughter …
A strong woman
is both soft and powerful
She is both practical and spiritual …
A strong woman
In her essence
Is a gift to the world.
—Unknown

Let's get comfortable with—no, let's fall in love with—who we really are as women. Let's fall head over heels, hopelessly, madly in love with our hearts, our bodies, our souls, our minds, and all of our abilities.

Loving ourselves—that's a tall order for most of us. Ask us to love our partner or spouse—of course. Ask us to love our children? To the end of the earth! Love our family? Done. Our friends? No problem. But loving ourselves to the same degree as we love and demonstrate that love to others—now, that's a problem.

Showing ourselves love each day, speaking to ourselves in a loving way, and embracing our flaws can be one of the most difficult challenges we face on our path to finding and embracing our authentic selves. But know this: we cannot find inner peace or live an enlightened life without loving ourselves. What's more, we cannot fully love another as a partner in this life—until we first learn to love ourselves.

Some of us don't ever feel beautiful, so we put up walls around us to protect ourselves. They can be in the form of extra weight, to create a barrier or an excuse as to why no one could ever find us attractive. They can be through sexual promiscuity, without ever giving our hearts so that we can feel wanted, but still in control. It can also be found by creating an implied distance, not allowing ourselves the opportunity to create personal connections in our lives for fear of hurt, rejection or abandonment.

Some of us may feel attractive, but it has gotten us into trouble in the past ... with men who wanted only our beauty and not our hearts. Some of us have used our beauty to get what we want: in the workplace (a smile at just the right time might get them to agree with you), among our friends (because everyone wants to be friends with the pretty girl), and certainly with lovers.

None of these examples draw us closer to our real beauty or acknowledge the gifts God has placed within us.

Most women I know, myself included, spend most of their days completely oblivious to their beauty. We have no idea how much beauty we bring to this world just by being in it ... not as an art form to be admired, but as a contributing heart and mind and spirit.

To begin, love yourself. Love all of yourself. Love the imperfections on your face;
the squishy parts of your tummy and thighs;
your smile lines around your mouth and your eyes; and
your precious heart—even when it's broken ... love it.

Love your mind.
Adore your giving, thoughtful, generous spirit.
Love your ability to care for others when they need you.
Remember the way you cry in a sad movie or along with a friend who's hurting.
Love your vulnerabilities, your insecurities, your shortcomings, and your many weaknesses. They're a part of you.

When you begin to love all the things that make you who you are, you also are able to see
your imperfect but beautiful body that can move and physically gets you through each day with grace;

your smile that tells the tale of all the joy and laughter in your past, present, and optimistic future;
your mind that has solved a number of last-minute science projects for your kids;
your creativity that created that amazing Thanksgiving dinner for family and friends;
your confidence and conviction when you see others being mistreated; and
the fire in your eyes when you are challenged.

The people in your life that take the time to know and experience all that you are will get
your heart;
your love and your hate;
your joy and your pain;
your light and your darkness;
your generosity and your selfishness;
your confidence and your moments of insecurity; and
your peace and your truth.

Love Lessons in Truth

As women we carry a lot on our shoulders, mostly because we can. But we have to stop holding that bar so high that we live in constant disappointment. We cannot all look like Hollywood actresses; build the successful career; be the supermom; attend church, soccer games, PTA meetings, business dinners, networking events; keep up with friendships; be a loving, perfect wife—who also just happens to be a sexual dynamo. I can't do all that. My guess is that you can't either. But we try and inevitably we fail. Relationships suffer, our goals go unmet, commitments are broken, and people are let down. But one of the greatest travesties of that bar of perfection is that each time we fall short, we love ourselves a little bit less. We're so hard on ourselves.

But one of the greatest travesties of that bar of perfection is that each time we fall short, we love ourselves a little bit less.

When someone pays us a compliment about the amazing presentation we gave at work, are we more likely to say, "Thanks, but I thought I went too fast, and I missed that one really important point," or just a simple "Thank you"? When a friend compliments us on how nice we look, most of us respond with, "Oh, thanks, but girl, don't you think it makes my butt look the size of Mount Rushmore," rather than a simple "Thank you."

Next time, you step out of the shower (be brave now), look at yourself in the mirror. Stop to admire the curves around your waist and hips. Notice the grace and beauty in the scars or markings you have from giving birth to your children. When you speak about your body, try to not begin with its imperfections.

I wonder what it would feel like to just "be" for one minute, one hour, or one day with no self-criticism or judgment—just gratefulness for and contentment with myself as I am right now.

I wonder how I would feel about myself if I committed to never saying another remark to myself that I wouldn't speak to my best friend.

I wonder what would happen if I saw myself as others see me. While we tend to view ourselves through our head (logic and judgment), we are much more likely to see others though the lens of our heart (love and compassion). We are more loving toward others than we are toward ourselves. We're often able to acknowledge people's imperfections but still rejoice in their lives. But we don't extend ourselves that same grace.

The same woman who offers me her strength describes herself as weak and broken. The woman who would never encourage her own daughter to accept disrespect in a relationship willingly does so in her own. The woman whom everyone else looks at and sees beauty sees something very different in the mirror each day. We've also all experienced those women that don't fit the typical profile for what constitutes "beautiful" in our world (the measuring stick of the models on magazine covers), but they're so full of spirit and joy and love that their beauty and energy is almost magnetic, and they *do* see their beauty—as a matter of fact, they embrace it!

Here's a radical thought: What if we began to see ourselves through the eyes of our Creator? The same Creator who made the heavens and the earth, the Caribbean Sea, and the Italian countryside also made us. He made us different intentionally; He didn't make a mistake.

He also gave us all the desires we have in our hearts right now. The desire to be appreciated—God placed it there. The desire to be seen and to be known—God placed it there. The desire for peace and happiness—God. That desire for love—our Creator.

No one can give us this gift of love. Genuinely loving ourselves is a gift that only we can truly give to ourselves. But doing so is dependent upon the image of ourselves we carry around, our self-worth and what we choose to see. Either consciously or unconsciously, we make a daily decision whether we will embrace all those experiences and characteristics that have created us into the fabulous women we are today. As disappointed as we may be in some of the things we are not, we need to begin rejoicing in all that we are. As sad or heartbreaking as some experiences may have been for us, we need to embrace them. We must recognize all these things for the lessons that they are and for what they have brought to our lives. Without them, our hearts and souls wouldn't be what they are today. You wouldn't be who you are at your core today ... a gracious, strong, kind, loving, blessed, grateful, imperfect, powerful, beautiful, loved, and worthy woman.

Life Lessons in Truth

You are not perfect, but you are trying to live better, and God looks at your heart. He sees the inside, and He is changing you little by little.
—Joel Osteen

CHAPTER 15

Here I Am

Love me when I least deserve it, because
that's when I need it the most.
—Swedish proverb

There have been many times in my life—more than I care to count or admit—that I am not proud of my choices. Looking back at my younger years, I can point to very specific times when I could look at myself from an outsider's perspective and simply shake my head in disbelief. I know that person; I'm familiar with her, but sometimes it's hard to not look away. I know her heart and her intentions, even if she lets me down periodically.

My catastrophically poor choice in men has a long and tenured history. I became sexually active at far too young an age; my first encounter was with someone older than I who, in today's world, could have gone to jail for taking advantage of the intense crush I had on him in the way that he did. I was in high school, he was in college. I had known him for years.

One of my first real boyfriends dropped out of high school, worked at Burger King, and cheated on me at the ripe old age of seventeen, with a woman who already had three children. It wasn't long after that breakup that I began seeing his older stepbrother, who was ten years my senior. Seriously? Just wait; it gets worse.

After college, one of the first relationships I entered into was with my boss at my first job. Don't say I didn't warn you.

It was around that time that I had decided I was going to find a nice young man. It was a few years after that decision that I met Jason, who is now my ex, as you know.

After my divorce, as I've mentioned, I fell in love with a narcissist, then was with a married man, and proceeded to date a series of men who meant nothing to me, nor I to them until I finally just stopped and let God go to work.

That pattern that I repeated throughout my life would be laughable, if it weren't so sad. I was going to continue to make poor choices in relationships until I faced some harsh truths about myself and found my own inner wisdom.

There were probably a lot of people that would have said that I was destined to repeat that cycle, continuing to make damaging choices when it comes to my heart for the rest of my days. They could realistically have said, "That's just how she is." I believe we all have an inner voice, and although mine had likely been speaking to me for decades, I obviously chose to press the mute button. I made poor choice after poor choice through my adult years, even after I was old enough to know better. And yet, after all that, here I am.

I have been able to identify and articulate, acknowledge and grieve all of my mistakes, all the ways I've placed myself and my heart in harm's way. I also made the conscious choice to learn from those past mistakes and to break that cycle in my life. I am no longer that person, telling all those lies to myself in order to justify my destructive behavior. I had to learn and grow, evolve and change. I had to hold myself accountable, and ultimately I had to forgive myself and those who had hurt me. No one could have done all that for me; it's a journey that is unique to each of us, and we have to find our own way through it.

I am no longer that person, telling all those lies to myself in order to justify my destructive behavior.

People can change; but people have to want to change. They have to be able to see it and want it for themselves. I've never seen an example of someone who has changed by the sheer will and determination of someone else.

Think about all the things you would like to see changed about a person you love. Maybe you're in a relationship that you would like to be more loving. Maybe someone you're close to has an addiction or a bad temper, or works long hours or doesn't take care of their health. Your wanting those changes for them or for your relationship with them will not make it so. There is likely very little you can do or say to that person that will make them change if they are not seeking change for themselves and for their own reasons. As a matter of fact, your attempts to change that person (and ultimately, by the way, control that person) may only push them further into their own personal abyss.

Consider all the times that someone has tried to change you against your will. How did that work out?

I know someone whose brother had a pretty significant addiction to prescription drugs. His sister and his children desperately wanted him to stop and thought that their love would be enough to make him seek help. Sadly, it was not, and he has spent several long years unfortunately disconnected from his family.

Life Lessons in Truth

As was the case with me, learning from our mistakes isn't always a direct path to change. The journey is not always sequential, building on itself and never making the same mistake twice. With each misstep, we take pieces from each experience. Sometimes it takes several pieces fitting together like a puzzle, or sometimes we need to see that same puzzle piece again and again in order for us to see how it no longer fits in our lives. I had to make the same mistake more than once (let's be honest, more than twice) to finally learn what the universe was trying to teach me. But even after all that, here I am.

Sometimes, when we don't learn our lesson right away and we make the same mistake repeatedly, we can be pretty hard on ourselves. We might even succumb to the idea that we'll never change or that the pain that's in front of us is all we deserve. That's another lie. We all deserve to be happy and whole. We all deserve the effort to keep trying until we get it right, until we learn the lesson we're supposed to learn. God's not giving up on any of us, and although He sees our mistakes, He's faithfully adjusting His prosperous plan for us accordingly.

I wanted a change, but I didn't really know what I wanted to change into; I didn't know what I was really seeking, except clarity. I didn't know how to fill my own emptiness. At the time, I knew only that the way I was could not continue. I was drowning at one point, grasping at anything and nearly anyone that might be a life preserver to save me from the rapids. I knew I couldn't be whole, I knew I wouldn't find a meaningful relationship until I created and embraced real change. I also trusted that God was watching over me and that He had a greater plan for me and my life.

I have realized that in this journey, there really is no clear end or finish line. The lessons never end and the growth never ceases. My journey and my transformation continue. Although I will still make mistakes along the way, I know my way back to joy.

So now, here I am.

CHAPTER 16

Next, Next, Next

I may not have gone where I intended to go, but I
think I have ended up where I needed to be.
—Douglas Adams

I had been saying that I wanted to live an extraordinary life, that I wanted people in my life who challenged me and helped me grow and become better. I had been saying that I wanted the opportunity to have experiences where I could really feel God's love for me and marvel at all the beauty that surrounds me. I wanted to live my dream of a rich, full, honest, giving, simple, peaceful life. I had also been hoping for that "big love," one that was sincere, strong, and passionate.

I had spent at least a couple years attempting to create this for myself. I had better relationships with my parents, my family, and my friends that had stood by me during a very difficult period. I had fewer friends in my life now, but they were true, authentic, and inspiring to me. I took the initiative to find a new job where I was valued and heard and had the opportunity to grow professionally and grow the business. I had been exposed to professional executive coaching, and it had a profound impact on my work and my working relationships. I had even begun the book I had always talked about writing. I sold my big, suburban home and moved into a more manageable downtown condo to give me a completely different perspective. I had traveled to amazing destinations and had more than my fair share of once-in-a-lifetime experiences. I had met someone who was honest, giving, strong, protective, and passionate. I met someone capable of the love I was seeking. He loved me deeply, fiercely in his soul and demonstrated that through his words and actions every day.

So, why couldn't I be still, be content, for even a moment?

It was my single greatest learning through this journey. I had spent my life constantly striving, reaching, grasping for that next move, that next experience, that next position, that next person (or worse, continuing to look back). I had this false belief that whatever was "next" would surely make me whole. It would surely make me happy.

> I had this false belief that whatever was "next" would surely make me whole.

We all have this hole in us that were constantly trying to fill up with something. Love, success, money, food, possessions, friends, accolades ... you name it I've chased them all at some point in my life. And I know I'm not the only one for whom enough never seems to be "quite enough." We purchase a first home, and within five years we've upgraded to a larger home with more square footage in a better, more upscale neighborhood. We get that first car, and it isn't long before we move up in terms of features and brands. We get that promotion at work, and we quickly have our sights set on the next rung on that inconsequential, never-ending corporate ladder. We meet a trustworthy and loving man, but maybe there's somebody even better out there. It's as if we have an appetite that can't be satiated. It's as if we're scared to stop swimming for fear that we'll drown.

So many of us have this aching that there's something physical standing in the way of our own happiness: once I have more money, once I have a smaller waistline, once I own a home, once I get a new job, once I have that child I've been longing for, once my child makes the cheerleading squad or the football team, once my child graduates from college, once my mother approves of me, once my father tells me I am important ... then ... then I'll be happy. Then I will surely be content.

Life Lessons in Truth

All the things combined that I had been longing for wouldn't make me whole or happy or content or complete. I had to fill that hole for myself.

There is no beauty or peace or stillness in a heart that's constantly yearning, reaching, grasping and looking for what's next. If we don't recognize all the blessings we have today, we might miss the opportunity to be still, to be content, to be happy and bask in this moment of sunlight. We miss the gift of being fully present. We miss the blessing of knowing that all that we are and all that we have is, in fact, enough.

Once I understood that hole and the source of that need, I then knew I had the ability to recognize and accept it for what it was. I could shine a light on it for exposure, without giving it importance in my life. I could make the choice of how to heal that hole. I could even make the choice of how to fill it; I could fill it with love—God's love, love for myself, and love by and for others. The day I realized that truth was the day when it all became enough. That was the day my heart stopped reaching for what was next and came to know its own peace. I learned this later in my life, but I'm grateful to have learned it at all.

CHAPTER 17

The Voice

The truth is that meaningful change is a process. It can be uncomfortable and is often risky, especially when we're talking about embracing our imperfections, cultivating authenticity, and looking the world in the eye and saying, "I am enough."
—Brené Brown

According the Mayo Clinic, women are nearly twice as likely as men to experience depression. Girls begin to hear their inner voices at an early age. In school we start to see boys look at another girl, and we think, *I'm not pretty enough*. We experience other kids getting better grades, and we begin to think, *I'm not smart enough*. We try for the lead role in the school play, and when we don't get the part we say to ourselves, *I'm not talented enough*. Then we hear our parents say, *Why can't you be more like your sister?* and we realize we've somehow disappointed the people we love most in this world and begin thinking, *I'm not good enough*.

Those voices get louder in early adulthood, as we try finding our way into a career where we can feel comfortable, and into a relationship where we can feel secure. As time goes on, those voices begin screaming at us from the board room to the bedroom: *You don't have what it takes. You're too assertive [you're a bitch]. You're not assertive enough [you're a pushover]. You'll never be as successful as the man sitting next to you. You'll never be as good as she is.* We allow those voices a prominent place in our daily existence, but those are voices from our heads. The noise from our heads tells us about all the things we think we've learned along the way, primarily from watching and comparing ourselves to others. Those voices tell us lies.

The voices from our hearts have a very different story to tell us. If we listen to our guts, our hearts, our spirits, our souls, we will hear a very different message. We will hear what we innately know but don't give a microphone to very often. We hear that because of our past experiences, we are competent and skilled and well equipped to thrive in our respective professions. We understand that we deserve a man that respects and honors who we are. We sense that we are beautiful inside and out—not in spite of our experiences, but because of our experiences.

> We sense that we are beautiful inside and out—not in spite of our experiences, but because of our experiences.

Those are our personal truths. We can tell the difference in these messages because they originate from a different place. They come from the heart, not the head. They originate from within us, not within others. But we can't hear the truth unless we quiet the noise. Once we find the peace within ourselves and really listen to what we hear, paying close attention to what we feel, we can sense what is true for us. Once we find it, we have the opportunity to tap into it as the need arises. That quiet voice from the heart is always there.

I have confessed more through this book than I expected to. I have bared all of my destructive decision making, my horrific choices, my numerous flaws and insecurities on these pages. There are words in here that no one in my family has ever heard me utter, and many of my friends wouldn't have ever guessed. It has taken a long time to allow me to experience forgiveness for myself, for my own shortcomings. That didn't happen of my own doing; I had to see myself through the eyes of my Creator to truly find forgiveness. I had to see myself as a child of God.

God knows my heart. Nothing that has occurred in my life is a surprise to God. He knew all this even before I was born. It's not as though He has been sitting up in heaven shaking His head at me saying, "What went wrong with this one? How could she have been so stupid?" No, I actually believe that God is not surprised at all. I think He has been looking down on me, smiling. Smiling that all-knowing, all-encompassing, all-forgiving, unconditional, patient smile for a young daughter when she has gone astray. He knew all this was going to come to pass for me; He knew what decisions I would make and the hurt I would feel and the hurt I would cause. And He knew I would find my way back.

Please don't misunderstand. I am not saying that God created the pain I experienced or that He willed these events to occur in my life. What I'm saying is that He knew the circumstances and influences I would be faced with, and because He gave me free will and He knows my heart, He knew how it would all play out. And through it all, He never turned away from me. He just stayed there like a patient father, looking over the horizon, waiting for me to come home to Him.

I was broken. I am certainly flawed. I worry over little, insignificant things. I'm not great with managing my money. I trust too easily and sometimes get taken advantage of by others. For as many weaknesses as I have, I have just as many, if not more, gifts. I am smart, introspective, generous, a hard worker, driven, caring, funny (or at least I think so), and forgiving. I have a high energy level and can accomplish a great deal when I put my mind to it. I am also a happy person and find a great deal of peace and fulfillment in helping other women find their own voices. I not only know who I am but know whose I am: I am a child of God. I have His grace; therefore, I am forgiven. I have His love; therefore, I am enough.

I know there are those of you thinking, *You left your husband of nearly twelve years. Then you were with a married man! How can you possibly get up and look at yourself in the mirror each day?*

Believe me, I've had to answer that question for myself quite often over the years.

I also know there are some people reading this right now that are thinking, *That's nothing ... you have no idea what I've done. You have no idea the hurt I've caused to myself and others.*

You're both right. I made some mistakes, and so have you. This isn't a contest of mistakes, and there certainly is no trophy or finish line for the winner. None of us are perfect, and I don't know anyone who has lived their life mistake-free. We all need to learn the power of self-honesty, self-forgiveness, and self-love.

I was recently at a house-warming party, where a woman I know casually seemed somewhat distant and sad that evening. I didn't know much about her. I had worked with this woman previously, knew that she had several failed marriages in her past, knew that she enjoyed working out. After most of the people left the party, she was sitting outside with a mutual friend and me. She shared that she wished she could be more like us—wearing long sundresses, looking pretty, feeling confident. She said that she changed clothes four times that night before coming out. She tried on three summer dresses, but because she hates her legs, she decided on her usual go-to outfit: jeans. She shared that she doesn't feel pretty and had recently stopped dating because she thinks she's not feminine enough, not confident enough, not whatever enough. To look at this woman, you would think that she has the world at her feet, she's that attractive. But she doesn't see her beauty. I said she works out a lot, but really she teaches TRX—which is an intense core training regimen. She doesn't see her strength.

Sharon Pope

Life Lessons in Truth

We always seem to be our own worst critics: my hair is too curly, my hair is too straight, my legs are too fat, my legs are too thin; I'm not smart enough, not fast enough, not assertive enough, too assertive; I'm a bad mother, a distant friend, not pretty enough, not confident enough, not whatever enough.

If God knew us before we were born and made us just as we are—just as we are supposed to be—then isn't that enough? If He believes that we are perfect just as we are, why can't we see ourselves that way? Because we keep looking through our own eyes and our own lenses. We keep looking through our heads filled with comparisons and judgments. We need to start looking at ourselves (and others, for that matter) through His lens.

All of these insecurities and comparisons are surely holding us back in our relationships and in our lives. If we don't begin to accept ourselves, then we will likely have a difficult time making real connections with others. We won't be confident enough to open ourselves up to another heart. If we want healthy, loving, fulfilled relationships, it's time we begin to forgive ourselves and love ourselves more.

I believe I couldn't have had a healthy, loving relationship until I forgave myself for some of my actions. Prior to that, I walked around with a pretty heavy heart. I know that since I have begun forgiving myself—and it's a process—my relationships with others are deeper and more meaningful. I also tend to hold others and their transgressions a little more lightly, because none of us are perfect, and we certainly weren't put on this earth to judge. I am no one special. I am clearly no saint, and yet when I get really still and listen with my heart, I know that I am more than enough. And, my friend, so are you.

CHAPTER 18

Sometimes I Scare Myself

Ultimately we know deeply that the other
side of every fear is freedom.
—Mary Ferguson

I thought I was doing something pretty frightening. I was having dinner alone at an Italian resort in a remote part of Tuscany that I had traveled to by myself. Yes, I know; that's full of intimidating circumstances: traveling overseas by myself, not knowing how to speak the language (outside of *grazie* and *vino*), and dining out with only a book to keep me company. But I was feeling pretty strong emotionally and thought I was managing it all pretty well. So, I started to write a chapter that might inspire other women to try something new and do something that was outside of their comfort zones—maybe even take on a bit of an adventure—knowing that it would all be okay.

I had no idea what the subsequent days would hold for me.

From this safe and secure spa resort in the mountains of Tuscany, I traveled to Florence via train. I had never been on a train before, and let's just say it wasn't my most graceful moment. To begin with, I was trying to lift and haul my heavy bags on and off the fast-moving European trains in four-inch heels. You can imagine that I'm not one of those women that packed just a small bag to travel around Europe; I probably had a small bag for my shoes alone. I didn't know where to put my bags, because it's not terribly intuitive, and had no idea if I was in the right seat, hoping at least that I was on the right train.

When the train arrived in Florence, I saw a bustling city that immediately overloaded all my senses and screamed to me that

Life, Love, Lies & Lessons

I wasn't in Ohio anymore (or even Tuscany, for that matter). I made my way to my hotel via taxi and was escorted up to my very small, dark room. This change of scenery made me feel anxious, intimidated, scared, and lonely.

My initial plan was basically to hide in my room for a while. That seemed perfectly logical. But, as luck would have it, this small room had no minibar, room service, or TV. It had a small bathroom and almost no light. To be fair, it also had a window, but it was boarded over with exterior shutters, so in my mind, that didn't count. It's hard to stay in a small room with no window for very long, and after all, I was in Italy. So, I gave myself some breathing space and allowed myself to feel fearful but did not allow myself to stay in a bubble. I told myself to "put my big-girl pants on"—to jump right in the deep end—and explore this damn city. So, off I went.

I grabbed my map with the sites circled on it that I had planned to see and ventured outside the hotel. Almost immediately, an Italian man began walking beside me and tried to either flirt with me or rob me. I wasn't certain which and was in no mood for either, so he quickly went away. It was late in the afternoon, and the closest of the attractions I wanted to see was the statue *David*. I walked several blocks, proud to have found my way, and waited in line for about forty-five minutes. I got in just before the museum closed and viewed the most amazing works of art I had ever seen. I had conquered my first expedition! This gave me the little bit of courage I needed to tackle another one: finding dinner. I found a place to eat outside in a busy square and ended up making friends with the waitress. She said they would be partying later and that I should come back and join them. Although I was feeling a bit more confident, I wasn't that brave—or stupid. I'd had enough excitement for one day.

There was one thing on my list that I knew I had to do while in Florence, and that was go to the Piazza Michelangelo. I had been told that it was an experience and a view of the city not to be missed. So the next morning I grabbed my map again, put on the most sensible shoes I had with me, and began walking. I was still very anxious and not at all comfortable. It was then that I really wished someone had come along with me on this trip. I was lonely, introspective, and more than a little sad. I had a flood of emotions coming at me: insecurities about my past, fears about my future, feelings of being unworthy of love and lacking direction.

The piazza was probably a three-mile walk from the hotel in the center of the city, up some winding and steep streets. I climbed hundreds of steps, and there, at the top, the entire city of Florence opened up below. It was incredible. It was breathtaking. It was peaceful. I sat in that place for hours, inspecting the city, watching people, trying to just settle my heart a bit. I sat at a little café and had a glass of wine and some cheese; I had earned it after all those steps. I sat. I wrote in my journal. I cried. I took probably a hundred photos. I walked some more to change my view of this expansive city. I watched a couple get their wedding pictures taken. I got still. I breathed deeply. I even bought some cheap souvenirs.

On my last full day, I knew I couldn't be left alone in the city to simply explore on my own, given my state of mind, so I made arrangements to go on a tour where I visited Siena, Pisa, a vineyard, and San Gimignano. I met some nice people on that trip, and being in a guided group put my heart a bit more at ease and left me little time for thinking too much or feeling too lost. Although my head was in the game that day, my heart surely was not. Regardless, I saw some amazing cities and faced some fears that I wasn't certain I was strong enough to push through. So, I saw that portion of my trip to Italy for the blessing that it was.

Life Lessons in Truth

During that part of the trip, I learned that Florence wasn't as big as I had originally thought, and I could find my way around without too much trouble. That gave me enough confidence to keep going. If I could make my way to the museum to see *David*, then maybe I could make my way to Piazza Michelangelo on my own. If I could eat at a village restaurant off the beaten path, where not a soul spoke English, then maybe I could conquer yet another train ride. I learned that it's important to recognize the state of your mind and your emotions and, when necessary, treat yourself with great care. I learned that in order to live authentically and honestly, I would experience a whole range of emotions and that they wouldn't all be good all the time—and that's okay. I learned that I do not have to be that woman who has to have it all together, all the time. I've learned that in reflection, there is tremendous growth. I learned that if I will just open my eyes to my surroundings, I have the potential to experience beauty and magnificence that I couldn't have ever imagined. I learned that even when I'm weak, I am stronger than I give myself credit for. I learned that uncomfortable experiences carry the potential to dramatically enlarge my vision.

> I learned that even when I'm weak, I am stronger than I give myself credit for.

I prayed a lot during this trip, since He was the only that spoke my language. Primarily, my prayer was: *God, please continue watching over me, and keep me safe. Help me to be present and to learn whatever lesson it is I am here to learn.*

While I was in Florence, I was scared of who I was, where I was, and what experience was around the corner, and scared that the feeling of brokenness I carried with me might never be completely healed. But I did it. And I would do it again.

Looking back on the experience now, I have a slightly different perspective on the famous Eleanor Roosevelt quote: "Do one thing every day that scares you."
Challenge yourself.
Push yourself to have deeper, more meaningful experiences.
It doesn't mean you have to terrify yourself. It doesn't mean you have to travel around the globe by yourself.
Start small, but start.

Do something that's outside of your routine of daily life.
Turn off the television for a night and pick up a book.
Pick up the phone and call someone you have avoided speaking with but deeply miss.
Send someone a card rather than a text or an e-mail.
Take a class.
Go for a walk and marvel at the beauty that's all around you.
Sit in a park and breathe deeply.
Go listen to live jazz, and pay close attention to the vocalist; a good, soulful singer will make you feel things you never have before.
Invite to lunch someone whom you've worked with and would like to get to know better. Assume you will learn something new from them.
Do a yoga, Pilates, or basic stretching class.
Have dinner alone.
Go see a movie alone.
Run a 5K or train for a half-marathon.
Say you're sorry.
Tell the truth to someone about how you're feeling.
Take a trip alone (even if it's only for one overnight) ...or be crazy enough to go to a foreign country alone.

The truth is that it doesn't matter what it is that we do, but rather that we do something. It turns out that life requires us to actually live. There's growth there, regardless of the choice. I see far, far too many people living out their lives on Facebook, lamenting their days, wishing there was more. The fact is, there *is* more. There is so much more, but we have to be open to the experience. Sometimes it means we're going to be fearful; other times we might be scared out of our minds. But if we set that fear aside and trust that we're being protected, the blessings are incredibly abundant. Purposefully and deliberately making a practice of doing things that scare us will enlarge our thoughts about who we are and all that we're capable of becoming.

CHAPTER 19

New Neighbors

You urgently believe that these people must be persuaded to see things your way, condone your true path, and grant you their heartfelt blessing. While their hard-heartedness is their problem, your inability to detach is yours. It's based on a childlike desperation to control the uncontrollable.
—Martha Beck, *Finding Your Own North Star*

Imagine you've been living in this small, dark house for a long time. The house fits right into the neighborhood, because many of the houses seem to have that same quality. The neighbors always have their curtains drawn and hardly ever come out of their house. When they do, they never look at you or speak to you. No one seems to have a pet, takes walks, or seems to grasp the value of a lawn mower and a well-kept yard. You feel isolated and depressed every time you think about it. One day it occurs to you that you don't have to stay in that house. You could go find another place to live that would be a more uplifting, positive, and healthy environment. So you relocate and move into a new house in a neighborhood that is clean, where the neighbors are friendly and welcoming. The day you move in, they're at your door with baked goods and bottles of wine (my favorite kind of neighbors!). You love it there ... until one by one, all the neighbors in your new neighborhood are being replaced by your old neighbors from your old neighborhood; they've somehow slowly purchased and moved into the homes around yours.

This would be similar to identifying and doing the hard work to heal our wounds but then continuing to spend time with family, friends, lovers, or even work associates who were the ones that created or perpetuated the hurt in the first place. We think we will be able to handle those existing relationships; we'll be able to help them see how much we've grown and maybe even get them to acknowledge the pain they caused in our lives. They'll finally tell us how proud they are. Through our own transformation, they will somehow be inspired to change themselves. Although I suppose all things are possible, I wouldn't hold my breath.

The work we do is our work for ourselves and our own healing on our own journey. So be careful not to get this twisted. For them to become whole, healed, and happy in their own lives, they would need to do their own work. And sadly, many people live their whole lives without ever going on that journey for themselves. As we know, it's hard to face those demons.

> For them to become whole, healed, and happy in their own lives, they would need to do their own work.

Our old neighbors that have followed us to our new neighborhood are our disapproving family members, existing friends, ex- or current loves that hurt us, or people at work that harbor nothing but negativity. And I know I didn't make the move away from all those neighbors to a new life in a new neighborhood just to create new memories of pain, disapproval, and hurt. Did you?

So, then, why is it that we continue to allow those who hurt us to have a prominent place in our lives? Why are we so fearful that we put our heart in harm's way rather than be alone?

There are essentially two solutions: we can either establish some ground rules for ourselves or find some new neighbors.

There will certainly be people in your life—particularly loved ones and family members—who will remain in your life. There may be no way around it. But we may be able to control how often we see them, under what circumstances, and how we allow ourselves to be treated by them. We can make a point to limit our interactions. (As the rulers of our own lives and our own happiness, we can give ourselves permission to not attend every family function.) Before these interactions, we become very intentional about how we will interact with them and plan for what to do if judgment or discouragement ensues.

The point of continuing these interactions absolutely cannot be to try to change them, their opinions, or their behaviors. Let me repeat: we need to accept that our interactions with those who hurt us are not for the purpose of convincing them to see the situation through our lenses. We do not require their verbal validation of our wound in order for it to be real. These interactions will only become more strained if we enter into them with the intent to try to change the person, particularly if they don't know or accept that they hurt us in the first place. We cannot control someone, we cannot change someone, and just as we want to be accepted as we are, so do they. They are hurting too (even if they don't recognize it); otherwise, they wouldn't have caused us the pain originally.

So if we accept that we cannot change them, and we cannot get them to accept or own their part in our pain, but we want them to remain in our lives, we need to establish some well-defined boundaries to keep ourselves whole. We need to be intentional about not allowing those who hurt us to hurt us further.

But there will be those that simply cannot remain. The damage was too great or the price of a setback more than we're willing to risk. Those are the souls that we will need to gently step away from. There's no need to make it dramatic or even to make them aware of it, but we do need to make a conscious decision to remove them from our lives. We can no longer see them, spend time with them, or allow them access in any way (yes, that includes "unfriending" them on Facebook).

There's a woman I have known for years. Recently I found out that as a child she had been repeatedly sexually abused by a family member. Her parents are pillars of their church and their community. Even though her parents are fully aware of what occurred, to this day, when she goes home for family dinners, she is forced to sit right next to this family member at the dinner table. It's as though if the damage done is ignored, then it never really happened, and they never have to face the truth of something so horrific. If they don't acknowledge or validate the pain of their own daughter, then no one will ever know, and no one will ever think less of them. I'm no psychologist, but that seems to me like a relationship that has to be amputated, immediately, regardless of what else may be lost in the process. That may mean that you don't often get to see some of your other family members that you love, or without some significant effort on your part. It may mean that you feel like an orphan or a traitor. There's always a cost, but in a situation as damaging as this you cannot deny yourself the sanity, respect, self-love, and care you so deeply deserve. That also is a high cost to bear. True healing will never fully occur if those relationships remain.

Other situations aren't as intense. During the months and years following my divorce, there have been both friends and family members that have simply opted out of being involved in my life. For some of those people, I believe that the breakdown of my marriage scared them, by placing doubt in their minds about their own relationships. Others may have simply recognized the person I was becoming and they liked the old Sharon better. There have also been people, including those that I deeply miss, whom I have had to simply walk away from in order to stay healthy.

Just as people evolve, so do relationships and change isn't always a bad thing.

Sharon Pope

Life Lessons in Truth

Finding new friends and neighbors can feel like a lonely place, but know that it's only temporary. Here's what I've found: the people I need in my life now—those who inspire me, challenge me, and help me become better—find a way of presenting themselves. And everybody else has simply fallen away. I have made many new friendships. It's as though the happier I get, the more friends I make. It's because as we become better human beings, we become a magnet for other good people, or people that need our energy. The people in my life either add or detract value and health. Those that detract value or diminish health are those with whom I establish my personal boundaries or move neighborhoods to find some new neighbors.

There will be those that make the transition with us in a supporting and loving manner, but many won't. Identify those relationships in your own life; although it will take some time, you ultimately will find yourself surrounded by people that lift you up and help you reach the very best version of yourself.

CHAPTER 20

The Glorification of Busy

Don't be afraid of death, be afraid of an unlived life. You don't have to live a life forever, you just have to live.
—Natalie Babbitt

In my greatest moments of clarity, I can see the core difference between my pre- and postawakening life: it is that I now want every part of my life to be extraordinary. It is no longer enough to be in a relationship that could best be described as "semihappy." It has never been enough to be in a career that's uninspiring but pays the bills, working alongside mediocre people doing average things. I'm not interested in having many friends to somehow fill a void in my life and occupy my time or distract me from my own reality; I now want connection with real people with real cares, real loves, real concerns, real hearts, and real contributions to a friendship. I'm not inspired by the thought of living an ordinary life.

There was a time in my life when I was not living, but I sure was busy. I wasn't unhappy, but I had no joy in my life. I was a self-professed master of juggling all the elements of my life, moving and doing from the time I woke up to when I laid my head down at night. I never took the time to get really still. I've been in that very busy place, and I'm not going back.

Women, by nature, are giving people. It's how we are built; it's what we are intended to do. We also are pretty good at multitasking, although I'm not sure we're intended for that. We have high expectations of ourselves, and those expectations are what drive us to do more, achieve more, and become more.

We glorify the effort, wearing the "busy badge" proudly, as if the last woman standing gets some prize. We revel in being busy, and the busier we are, certainly the better wife, mother, professional, friend, and daughter we are. We take care of the needs of our children, our significant others, our parents, our neighbors, our friends. We attend parent–teacher conferences, go to all the children's sports events, driving them all over town for the practices and games, and help them with their homework. We attend church and hold seats on church committees. We keep the social calendar for the family, plan vacations and birthday parties, take care of the home, the laundry, the cleaning, the grocery shopping, the meal preparations, the pets. We make sure to visit our parents and share our lives with them. When a friend is in need, we come running. We give our whole selves at work for that sense of accomplishment, to prove our worth or sometimes just to pay the bills.

But in the midst of all that giving, I fear we've lost track of our hearts.

How are you being fed spiritually and emotionally? How do you keep your tank from coming up empty when you lay your head down at night? How is that sustained over time, and what toll has it taken? What have you given up of yourself along the way? What have you sacrificed in your own relationships, your own health, or your own happiness? Are you more alive or less alive as a result of all that giving?

My guess is you read over those questions without really answering them for yourself. Part of the work we are called to do on this journey to authenticity is to allow ourselves the opportunity to answer significant questions and feel our emotions. On this journey, we don't get to just by-pass or suppress every emotion and then pretend that we're healed. Just as we can't avoid those pesky emotions, we also can't wallow in them. The journey through truth requires us to feel it, then heal it. We cannot heal what is unspoken, unacknowledged, or unfelt.

> The journey through truth requires us to feel it, then heal it. We cannot heal what is unspoken, unacknowledged, or unfelt.

Allow me to introduce you to my friend Anne. Anne is an intelligent, hardworking, professional woman that has worked her way up to "sitting at the big boys' table" at one of the largest professional services firms in the country, as senior vice president in the accounting department: no small undertaking. Her daughters see that ambition in her and, I believe, dream bigger for themselves as a result. Although Anne could certainly use her high-stakes job as an excuse for missing some of her kids' activities, she never does. She still attends virtually every game, meets all the parental obligations that come with being a sports mom, and takes care of their physical needs and the home. She is a single mother; she wants to stay in touch with her friends and establish a relationship with a man.

Now, my dear friend Anne is no superwoman; she's probably a lot like you. She lives day-to-day and does all that she can. I don't think she has a single idea as to how to stop the gerbil wheel that she's on, so she just keeps running. Her needs always come last, and most of the time, they're just not even on the long list that gets accomplished each day.

I can see doing that for a "sprint," but life is more of a marathon than it is a sprint.

Anne is, to me, the perfect mother in almost every way; but she is not good to herself, and as a result she is not living a whole, healthy, authentic life. She is not emotionally or spiritually whole. She doesn't ask and answer the difficult questions. She believes that feeling emotions is a sign of weakness. She doesn't see or acknowledge her own beauty; she doesn't have time for that. She doesn't consistently have the time or energy to truly explore her own personal growth. She allows herself to stay in a relationship with a man that consistently demonstrates to her that she's not important, feeding the deeply rooted belief that treating herself (and her heart) with care is inconsequential. Anne hasn't healed some wounds ... but boy, is she ever busy!

Life Lessons in Truth

There is no road map on how to do this, no book you can buy that will somehow give you more hours in a day or less on your plate. I think women today are creating history with all the responsibility we have. If you think about it, there's never been another generation quite like the one we're in. It was only a few decades ago that we were fighting for the right to vote and to serve in the church; several decades ago, our parents didn't live long enough to need care at the same time that we were raising children (creating the "Sandwich Generation"). Women are now having children later in life, after their career is more established and therefore more demanding. We're still fighting for equal pay in the workplace, but the demands on women have grown exponentially. Now, our kids are not just in one sport but multiple sports, and it requires them to compete all over town almost every day of the week. Women today, more than ever, have so many expectations placed upon us that it's virtually impossible to live a "whole life" without a significant degree of intentionality.

We all have to choose what's important for each of us to be happy and healthy in our lives, in our relationships, and everyone's choices will be different. When we prioritize our daily list, we simply cannot put our own needs on the perpetual back burner and hide every emotion. The thing we may need the most to feed our soul may be a candlelight bath one day, and it may be making snow angels with the kids on another. Inserting joy into our lives shouldn't be an extravagance.

We think that the more we do, the better we are, but that's a lie. The more we heap on our plates, the less opportunity we have to really do anything well. For example, if your tank is completely empty when you get home from work at 8:00 p.m., but your kids need help with their homework, are you going to be fully present for them? Maybe you'd like to be able to connect to your husband but simply don't have the energy left, and you both fall asleep on the couch during *The Late Show*. Is your relationship better or worse as a result?

One of the options available to us is to accept help in our lives. I know this is probably blasphemy, but children can pick up after themselves, do the dishes, or even do their own laundry. My niece has been doing all the laundry in their house for years. Our husbands might be able to get dinner ready (or at least order it and set the table), but that might require us to be okay with him doing that in a different way than we would have done. Sometimes, we can be our own worst enemies, because we want to check all these boxes at the end of every day, but we also want them completed in our way at our time. One of the best investments I ever made was hiring someone else to clean my house. I'm not good at it, and it would take me all day to do what a pro does in two hours. Now, I have time every week that I've freed up to do something that I love and that feeds my soul.

Lastly, we need to give ourselves a break and lower that bar a bit. The bar height is created by us. Almost without exception, *we* are the ones placing those expectations on ourselves. We need to show our daughters what living looks like and give ourselves permission to breathe.

Giving is what we were meant to do, but it's not all we were meant to do. Placing others' needs before our own is the natural, unselfish act that we're built to do; but it's not fulfilling all that we're capable of or called to do. We are capable of so much more. We are worthy of so much more. We are called to become so much more. We may not be able to do it all, but what we choose to do, we can do well and with great love. We can raise wonderful children and grow into a whole life for ourselves. We can allow ourselves to feel emotions without getting lost in them, without judgment, and without associating them with weakness. We can live. We can live extraordinary lives. We can live big, massive, meaningful, tremendous and yes, peaceful, joy-filled lives.

CHAPTER 21

Get Real

Perhaps strength doesn't reside in never having been broken,
but in the courage to grow strong in the broken places.
—Unknown

I had moved and was getting to know a group of people that were new to me. People were friendly enough, but it was a bit of a superficial dance that was taking place: them seeing if I would be able to fit into their group and get the steps right, me stepping onto that dance floor only long enough to see if I could trust them. Then one day something interesting happened that completely changed the dynamic of the whole group: someone shared something personal about themselves and their life, something they had been struggling with for a long time. All of a sudden, the walls came down around the group. People began to open up a bit and see one another through a softer lens.

Once someone shares a piece of themselves, the ice thaws and a community begins to be formed through connection. All it takes is that one person to make themselves vulnerable to another, and it starts a domino effect, creating an environment for openness and honesty. It creates an environment where real conversations can take place, where real lives are shared, and where real hearts are opened. Once we can be our authentic selves with one another, healthy relationships can begin.

When people have the courage to share something deeply personal about themselves with us, it is a gift; it shows that they trust us. They trust us to not judge them. They also trust us to hear them; so many people in this world just simply want to be heard. That gift they've given us may start small, wrapped up tight in a little box with a yellow ribbon wrapped around it. But if we unwrap it carefully and keep it secure, those gift boxes will get bigger and bigger, with more elaborate wrapping. The interesting thing is that the biggest of gifts is typically the smallest of secrets that have been hidden away in the corner of someone's soul for a long time. When we receive that gift from another, we need to cherish it and treat it with great love. Doing so demonstrates a healthy respect for their journey. Doing so will also open the door to further their self-discovery and healing. That's how we can nurture real relationships and help each other in this world. It can be as simple as listening, respecting, and loving.

At the core of being "real" is the ability to acknowledge our own imperfections and our brokenness. In order to be authentic, we have to be transparent, and that takes courage and vulnerability and a whole lotta faith. For most people, the acknowledgment of our flaws means that we're working on improving. Acknowledgment of the fact that we're imperfect beings (yes, it's true) can be tremendously empowering. The minute I stopped pretending that I had all the answers, I found the sense of freedom and authenticity I had been craving. For me, all it took was saying, "I don't know": "I don't know where this road is taking me. I don't know who I'm becoming. I don't know what tomorrow holds." The only thing I did know was that I had a power much greater than me who was watching and guiding my steps.

The fact that we can give a name to our struggles and talk about them with others means that we're open to working on them, open to healing that brokenness. That's part of what makes us real. It comes more from a place of humility than from ego, because it begins with the acknowledgment of our imperfections, our struggles, our scars, our brokenness, the desire to improve. We need to pull back the veil of secrets and start having real conversations about our "stuff" and the things that every woman experiences. We are not unique in our struggles; surely, we're not the trailblazer of every woman's challenges. As special as we are, we're probably not as unique as we think when it comes to our struggles. As we begin sharing what we're going through and sharing the tools that lighten our loads, we can create a community of real women helping one another. We also discover that we're not alone.

> We also discover that we're not alone.

In your life, you cannot heal what goes unspoken. You cannot fix what never gets acknowledged. We like to act like everything's fine, all the time. But sometimes things aren't fine. In those times we need to be able to name what's wrong, describe how we feel, and understand what would make us happy. If we can't understand and share those feelings in a nonjudgmental way with one another, then we will never get past them. Those wounds won't heal. We will carry them around with us like weights in our pockets through all of our days. We certainly won't find peace or authenticity in our lives.

Think about the woman you know who is "fine" all the time. Some people genuinely are at peace and happy in their lives; I'm not talking about those women. I'm referring to the woman who always claims to be fine but then walks around as if she's carrying the weight of the world on her shoulders, so you can tell that she's not being honest with herself or anyone else.

How many of us have become frustrated with our partner because we weren't getting what we needed in the relationship, but we didn't really tell him exactly what that was? Be honest, now. If you've ever been told, "I can't read your mind," then you're as guilty as the rest of us. Anytime we hold back from being completely honest and authentic with another person—particularly someone we care about—we are inviting sickness into the relationship. It leaves that person to misinterpret what you need or what you're trying to communicate, making assumptions that are typically inaccurate. The reason we hold back is fear. There's something we're afraid to share. For me it was a fear of admitting that I needed love and support, because then my first husband and everyone I knew would know I didn't have it all figured out. I wasn't ready to admit that to myself, much less anyone else.

Life Lessons in Truth

People who love us typically want to give us what we need. But most of the time, they simply don't know either what that is or how to do so. It would help both people in the relationship if at least one could just share in an open, honest, and humble way what it is they desire. We can share what's missing in our lives. We can share our dreams for the future and what it is we just cannot live without. It can be terrifying. But there's an opportunity for all of us to recognize the fear we're feeling, stroke it, love it a little, pat it on the head but set it aside, knowing we can always come back and pick it up later. And then go ahead and share that part of ourselves anyway with the people we love. Most of the time, our worst fears never come true. The stories we create about what could happen are always much scarier than the reality of what will actually occur. Our pride and ego might get a little bruised, but we can set those right next to our fears.

When did honesty become so dangerous? When did hiding our hearts become the safe way to live? It probably started the first time we were laughed at or rejected or made to feel unworthy. Every time that reoccurred in our lives, it reinforced the idea that it's dangerous to show people who we really are and what we really think and feel. It's unnerving to admit we either might be wrong or don't know the right answer, especially if people are looking to us for the answers. It's scary to admit what we're feeling personally or the pain that happened in our lives, because it will bring to the surface some things that we may not be ready to face. It's humbling to have to admit when we caused pain to either ourselves or others through our own actions. It's hard to say, "I'm sorry." But I've learned that I can't live an honest life and be true to who I am at my core if I live in fear of the things that I refuse to acknowledge. I can't have healthy, lasting relationships with the people that mean the most to me in this world unless I show myself to them.

Real flaws, real awareness, real conversations can all lead to real, authentic, powerfully self-aware individuals and deeply rewarding relationships. I believe we can all help one another along this journey.

CHAPTER 22

The Mirror and the Demons

If you hate a person, you hate something in him that is a part of yourself. What isn't part of ourselves doesn't disturb us.
—Hermann Hesse

Don't be intimidated by the word *demon*. Demons are simply those traits, habits, and insecurities that we all hang on to and struggle with: anger, impatience, arrogance, control, worthlessness, fear, judgment, inhibitions, mediocrity, shame, or addiction. We cannot change what we don't see, so it's important that we identify and get comfortable with our demons. It's important that we call them by name and claim them as our own. Don't be scared of demons; be scared of what you don't see, of what you don't know on a first-name basis. Those are the things that can harm us and our relationships, because we don't even realize they're something to contend with. In our hearts, we know what haunts us, what holds us back from being the best we're capable of becoming.

Name your demons. Mine are impatience, judgment, control, and lack of self-control. Believe me that the irony of thinking that I can control so many parts of my life and all the circumstances around me—except for my own actions—does not escape me. If it wasn't so ridiculous, it might be funny. For some reason, I think I can control both people and situations, but that I, at times, cannot seem to stop at the second glass of wine. What is that all about?

Maybe it's the controlling part of me, but I feel that if I'm aware of and speak about my demons, it gives them less power over my life. They may enter my mind, but they will not gain access to my heart. They may pull me down for a minute, but they won't keep me down, because I'm able to look them in the eye and call them by name. Doing so takes away their power over my life, my will, my actions.

> If I'm aware of and speak about my demons,
> it gives them less power over my life.

Have you ever noticed that we tend to gravitate toward others with demons similar to our own? It's comforting, isn't it? Sometimes it allows us to justify our demons, to perpetuate and reinforce the habits, knowing that we're not alone; other times, it provides that door to share and discuss that which we're trying understand and overcome.

Using the wine as an example, it was only a few years ago, when I was married to my first husband, that every college-football Saturday afternoon we would get together with a group of our neighbors in the suburbs to tailgate and enjoy the game. To be honest, the men enjoyed the game, while the women typically stayed in the kitchen catching up and visiting with one another. The festivities began early and lasted until late in the evening. If it was a 12:00 p.m. football game, the party began around 11:00 a.m.; beer would be flowing for the men, and there was always plenty of cheap wine for the women to enjoy. Everyone brought at least one dish to share, and the host usually made a main dish, so the food was nearly as abundant as the alcohol. We would be there for both the early game and the late game, typically going home around 9:00 p.m. that night. In that time, I would easily drink at least an entire bottle of wine, but there was one neighbor in particular that would always drink much, much more.

Linda was the woman that all the neighbors loved dearly but would talk about her behind her back regarding her drinking habits and behavior. It was all veiled in concern, but looking back, I wonder if there wasn't something more at work in those conversations. It didn't necessarily have to be a football Saturday for Linda to begin drinking before noon. Linda drank a lot, virtually every day, typically until either her husband poured her into bed or she passed out. She had part-time work occasionally and was never able to have children. Her contributions in the marriage were cooking and keeping up on the house, and she did an amazing job, keeping a beautiful home. She worked hard at it, and no one could clean like Linda. It could be a hundred degrees outside, but she would still be out there mowing the lawn and working in the flowerbeds.

There was one point in her life, when her husband was battling cancer, when the drinking was particularly bad, because she was truly, genuinely distraught.

But this story isn't actually about Linda, but rather about the rest of us sitting beside her.

The other neighborhood ladies and I would sit there with Linda all day, drinking alongside her, all the while making mostly silent judgments about how much she would drink. None of us ever discussed our own drinking patterns with one another, because we never thought there was anything wrong with us. Linda's habits gave the rest of us the luxury of being able to ignore how much we were drinking, because it always paled by comparison. All the rest of us—myself included—were drawn to one another because drinking and entertaining was something we all had in common and all enjoyed. We supported one another; we lied to one another.

It makes me wonder what would have happened if one of us had simply stopped drinking. My guess is that it would have caused a level of discomfort among the group—awkwardness at first, but genuine discomfort ultimately. Or what if Linda informed us that she was no longer drinking? I imagine we all would have needed to confront this demon for ourselves, because our excuse would have been taken away.

I think when someone breaks free from one of their demons, the other people surrounding them that share those same demons realize they no longer have a crutch that they can share with that person, a point of comparison or an excuse. The dynamic between people changes. There was a certain cadence, a rhythm before that is no longer there, and that dreaded mirror shows up. It forces us to look ourselves in the eye and answer the questions about our own demons. We justified these habits as long as other people were with us doing the same thing, or worse by comparison; it made it okay to perpetuate. Now, without someone else to compare ourselves to, are we the same people about whom we were gossiping? Surely not!

Maybe you've been the one walking away from a demon, and that same rhythm and cadence you had with friends and family changes all of a sudden. You're not exactly sure why, but they're treating you differently, holding you at arm's length. That doesn't have anything to do with you, my friend. That means they're struggling with their own mirror as a result of the changes and accomplishments you've made in your life. By you overcoming your demons, you've somehow impacted their lives by taking away their excuses. It's important that you stay on your path and do what's right for you and what brings you peace. Just be aware of the meaning behind the changes you'll experience in the dynamic you shared with friends and family.

Now, the story I told was one about alcohol abuse and to a certain extent, addiction. But this story could be about always buying more and more (homes, cars, handbags, jewelry, etc) to perpetuate a lifestyle that we believe somehow makes us "on par" with those we respect and admire. It could be parents who place their kids in way too many sports in an attempt to be accepted or worse yet, have your child somehow achieve all that you felt you lacked at their age. It could be the groups of women we enjoy an occasional cocktail with, bad-mouthing our husbands together, because even though we've taken away every ounce of his masculinity through our controlling, we're somehow shocked that he is still disappointing us in any number of ways.

I realize I may have hit a nerve there on at least one of those examples. If you felt some irritation while reading that, then something rang true for you that you weren't ready to hear. That, is a demon. Don't be scared, mad, irritated about something you can understand and call by name; be afraid of what you continue to brush under the rug and not acknowledge for fear of having to stare it down in your own mirror each day.

There was a time in my life when I had very little tolerance for people who showed emotional weakness. Jill was a young woman in my ex-husband's family that used to drive me absolutely crazy. I couldn't stand being around her and discounted nearly everything she said. She would get anxious and depressed, she was introspective and easily led by others and every conversation had to be deep and laborious. I am now able to see that the very qualities that irritated me the most about Jill were actually all my own demons in the mirror that I wasn't ready to face yet. It was I who was emotionally very weak, even though I would never allow anyone to see that in me. It was I who was introspective and actually had a lot to say, but I would have had to let people behind my barricade.

Life Lessons in Truth

When we get really honest with ourselves, we come to understand that the qualities in other people that irritate us, shake us or disturb us the most are the exact things we need to heal for ourselves. Who in your life right now frustrates you the most and why? That is your demon. Recognize it. Face it. Call it by name. Heal it if you can.

CHAPTER 23

Courage

Courage doesn't always roar. Sometimes courage is the little voice at the end of the day that says I'll try again tomorrow.
—Mary Anne Radmacher

I was paid an enormous compliment by a long-time friend. Claire and I had been friends for close to nine years, and during that time, we've seen each other through divorces, seen her only child enter and graduate college, lived through broken wedding engagements and ailing parents. It's a relationship that means a great deal to me, because I've learned and grown so much from knowing this woman. She is one of the strongest, most resilient, happiest women I know. I hold my relationship with Claire very gently, handling it with care and love. She and I went through a rough patch in our friendship that I wasn't certain could be mended. When she started dating after her divorce, I couldn't understand why she was dating men that didn't deserve her and kept hurting her. I viewed it as a sign of weakness, and that was during a time when I didn't have much tolerance for that. It wasn't until I experienced something similar myself, following my own divorce, that I finally understood how that could happen. It wasn't until I faced my own insecurities that I understood how our choice in men is a reflection of our own self-worth. I was able to see her experience through more compassionate eyes. I apologized to Claire and she forgave me; I'm blessed to say we're still friends today.

Claire and I tend to connect better when it's just the two of us and not a large group of women. While at dinner one night, we were sharing each other's hopes for the future, talking about things we had learned and dreams we still wanted to accomplish in our lives. It was in the context of that discussion that this incredible woman said to me, "You're the most courageous person I've ever known." Wow! That's a big, powerful statement, and while I appreciated the enormous gift, I wasn't sure what I had done to deserve it. It made me start to think about what it meant to live a courageous life.

The Merriam-Webster Dictionary defines courage as "mental or moral strength ... to persevere and withstand danger, fear, or difficulty."

Life Lessons in Truth

For me, courage means being willing to explore. We must be willing to explore the unknown in ourselves, to want to learn, to want to see new things and have new experiences, even when—most importantly when—they're outside of our comfort zone. Maybe it means having a natural curiosity about life, about others, and about ourselves. It means, sometimes, being able to be truly honest with ourselves, distinguishing between how things are compared to how we wish they were. It might mean peeling back the layers of the onion. It might mean occasionally going to some dark, quiet places where we wouldn't invite others.

Maybe living with courage is just getting through those dark times ... the guilt-ridden times when we realize we've made a mistake in our marriage and impacted the lives of many people in the process; the lonely times when we're going through a divorce in a family that believes that divorce is an eternal sin; the times when, as we try to find what we want in a relationship, we get hurt by those who tell us, "I love you," only to leave. We all have moments, days, weeks, years where we're down. It takes strength to pull ourselves through that guilt, shame, and loneliness to another place, where the edges are a little softer, the people a little more forgiving, the sad times not quite as dark. It takes courage to acknowledge, forgive, and heal old wounds, trusting that we will be okay through the process and will one day come to see the experience as a lesson that we wouldn't change.

I think courage can mean having faith in others. Placing our trust in another requires courage. It can feel a little risky, particularly when we risk our hearts. Just because somebody has let us down before, maybe even multiple times, does not mean that we have to shut ourselves off from ever trusting another. While it's true that some may let us down, others may surprise us. If we live our lives through those broad brushstrokes of fear, we can miss the beauty of living within a trusted space alongside an honorable soul.

I think living with a measure of courage means living with intention and heart. I have really put my heart into relationships, and sometimes it has backfired. I've been hurt, I've been lied to, I've been left behind to feel very unimportant by friends, by men, by family. But I simply don't know any other way to live. When I give someone my heart, they get my whole heart; most don't understand what that means, nor do they comprehend the enormity of what I'm entrusting to them. But I simply don't know how to love someone with just half a heart or a little portion of my heart. Is that how you would want to be loved? But it takes courage, doesn't it, to trust another human being with something so precious?

> I simply don't know how to love someone
> with just half a heart...

Maybe that's what my friend Claire meant. Maybe that's what she saw in me that caused me to explore that question in myself.

Maybe the quote at the start of the chapter says it all. Maybe some days it's just having the simple courage to try again and to attempt to get a little better, a little more confident, a little more secure, a little more daring, a little more thankful, a little more forgiving, a little more trusting, a little more loving, and a little more joyful each day.

CHAPTER 24

Light

You don't see it. He's stealing your light.
—Traci Snyder

There is a part of us that isn't physical—we can't ever touch it, yet it can be experienced. We can't see it, but it is beautiful. We can't hold it, but it holds our deepest longings and desires and is the expression of our truest heart.

It's the human spirit, the soul, or as I like to refer to it, the light inside us.

This light is expressive:

It is the beauty in our watery eyes when we cry because someone's words moved us to tears.

It is the excitement in our smile upon experiencing pure joy.

It is the strength we hold in our bodies through our ability to bring life into this world.

It is the compassion we show when we see another human being in need.

It is how our whole body looks at peace when we're holding a child's hand or reading them a book.

It is how we close our eyes when we're singing a song that holds tremendous meaning.

It is the glow on our faces when we're in love.

It is also the head-thrown-back-laughing-out-loud expression we have when we're among good, trusted friends.

That's our light. That's our deepest beauty, because it's the physical expression of our souls.

I believe the soul is the single greatest proof of a living God and that the soul gets expressed through an inner light. That light is a gift from God. Therefore, the soul, our light, is important. It needs to be protected, loved, nurtured, and appreciated.

> I believe the soul is the single greatest proof of a living God and that the soul gets expressed through an inner light.

On our journey to recognizing and knowing our authentic selves, there will be people that either intentionally or unintentionally will attempt to steal the light we have inside of us. There will be those that are envious, threatened, or simply hurting, so they try to hurt us.

> Has there ever been a time for you that a close friend diminished your achievements, rather than celebrating your joys alongside you? That lessens your joy.

> Has there ever been a man whom you let into your heart and he disrespected you, without ever having any real interest in pursuing or caring for your heart? That makes you feel unworthy and unloved.

> Do you have a family member who means well but continuously tries to put you in the box they live in,

that they feel safe in—because that's where they're comfortable? That makes you feel reckless or extravagant.

Have you ever been in a job with a manager who didn't value your opinion or truly give you the opportunity to contribute in any meaningful way, essentially telling you that you're not important? That diminishes you and makes you feel small.

Has there ever been someone important in your life who told you or implied that if you don't believe exactly as they believe or live your life exactly as they live, God doesn't love you—and you actually believed them for a moment? That's heartbreaking.

I have experienced these things. They hurt. They weakened me. They caused me to feel as if I were carrying a heavy weight around my neck, my shoulders a little hunched over and my head hanging a little lower. I favored clothes that were comfortable more than what looked good on me. My smile didn't carry as much joy, my eyes didn't sparkle, I looked and felt hollow; my light was dimmed.

Life Lessons in Truth

Rather than bringing themselves up to our level, it's so much easier for these "light-stealers" to try to bring us down to theirs—it requires no work on their part, no growth or new perspective. For most of them, their actions stem from their own sickness, their own pain, and their own insecurities. They're hurting; forgive them. They're broken too—we all are in our own ways.

I've always been a bit obstinate; just ask my mother. And protecting my own light is one area of my life where that willfulness has served me well. I might be dragged down for a little while, but I eventually am able to stand up for myself, see those "light-stealers" as they are. I am able to take the time to heal what was broken and move forward with my head held high, weights set aside, eyes sparkling, heart open again. I can do that because at my core, I know who I am, what I believe, and the value I provide in this world. It is God who gives me my sense of self. And if He has given me that gift, then who am I to allow someone else to try to squelch that or take it away?

Our light is a precious gift; protect it. Like any fire, all it needs is a little air to breathe and some occasional new kindling in order to keep burning. Our light is a gift and a reflection of our souls; love it, nurture it, embrace it, and let it glow brightly.

CHAPTER 25

Still

In the next moment, in the next hour, we could choose to stop, to slow down, to be still for a few seconds ... In the middle of just living, which is usually a pretty caught-up experience characterized by a lot of internal discussion, you just pause.
—Pema Chödrön, *The Power of Pause*

We go so fast. We expect so much of ourselves; whatever we do, we want to be good at it. Sometimes in the pursuit of unattainable perfection, however, we need to stop long enough to rest, to think, to get still and quiet, to heal, to restore, and to breathe. And we need to be alone to do it.

As you now know, I took a ten-day trip to Italy by myself. While I was there, I visited two spas—one in Tuscany and one in Lake Garda, in northern Italy. There were many, many moments on that trip that I was forced to be silent. For one thing, since I was by myself, I didn't have anyone to talk to, and for another, I didn't speak the language. But the absolutely breathtaking view of the Italian countryside also demanded a certain amount of reverence—simply out of respect and gratitude. I had some of the most impactful experiences of my life there when I was able just to be still, be quiet, and be open.

On my first morning, I woke up early, and before having breakfast, went straight to the spa area. I had made a reservation for their infinity-edge whirlpool, without any idea why I had to make a reservation just to use a whirlpool. Once I entered the whirlpool area, I realized why. Picture an enormous indoor pool, such as what you see in luxury resorts: four feet deep, with stages all around to provide heated water therapy to different parts of your body. That indoor pool led to an outdoor infinity-edge pool that also had the whirlpool features on the reclined seating within the pool overlooking the Tuscan countryside. And I had that entire pool—inside and outside—all to myself for thirty minutes. There was no music, no cell phones, and because it was early in the morning, there also were no voices to be heard in the distance. It was still and quiet and magnificent. This was my first full morning in Italy, so I struggled a bit with the "getting still" part, but certainly none of the beauty was wasted on me that day.

From there, I went out and sat by the cool pool. The cool pool was an outdoor pool that was separate from the spa's primary guest pool but still with an amazing view. The water was much cooler than the primary guest pool, which was heated. There was no one else around, probably because most people don't want to swim in cold water. It was so peaceful. I had plenty of time to get still, to think, to rest, to journal, to listen to my heart many mornings out by the cool pool.

In both of those instances, I was alone and it was quiet. In experiences like that, where we hold the ability to quiet our minds a bit, we can hear our hearts speak.

There were lunches and dinners at this spa that literally brought me to tears on more than one occasion. There was something about the freshness and simplicity of the food that stopped me in my tracks. I couldn't believe how something so simple could taste so good. It was worthy of taking it slow and enjoying every bite, every flavor, and every sip. I had never had meals like that before and have not since.

The second spa I visited was situated up on a cliff overlooking an enormous deep blue lake and, again, the Italian countryside. It was cooler up in the mountains at Lake Garda. This particular spa had a different version of having a dedicated pool for a period of time. I spent thirty minutes in a two-foot-deep saltwater pool in a softly lit room. Because the resort was built into the side of a mountain, many of the spa rooms were actual caves. There was no one there in the room with me, and all I had was an hourglass to help me know when time had elapsed.

I decided to not wear my bathing suit in the saltwater pool. I swam naked in a saltwater pool by myself for thirty minutes. This proved to be a very restorative, healing experience for me. I wasn't very proud of my body at that time, choosing to hide it in the spa robes more than the bikini. Swimming in saltwater felt different than swimming in pool water. Swimming with no clothes feels different than swimming fully clothed. I spent the time attempting to love my body a bit more and treat it with a little more kindness. I spent the time attempting to love myself a bit more and treat my heart with a little more kindness. In that time, I felt light and soft and beautiful, and I hadn't felt that way in a long time. There's a certain beauty to a woman when she stops loathing and reaching and striving to simply be at peace. There's a certain beauty to a woman who is able to get out of her own head and get in touch with her body and her heart.

One of the other restful and healing experiences at that particular spa was the waterbed room. Now, don't start thinking crazy stories. It wasn't anything perverse, and I will do my best to serve it justice through words. It was again a cavelike room where there was very little light. The floor was composed of large, flat rocks that you could walk on; otherwise, you would be stepping into running water. The beds were filled with water and elevated above the running water and rock floor. There was no music, there was no talking, and there certainly weren't any cell phones. I don't know how long I was in that room and on that bed that day several years ago, but I can tell you that during that time, I had peace. I had nowhere to go and nothing to do—no commitments, and this time, I had no time limit. So, I rested, I prayed, and I was grateful.

Sharon Pope

I went down to the bar one evening after dinner, ordered a cocktail, and listened to live jazz music. The singing was in English, and they played one of my favorite songs by Corinne Bailey Rae, "Put Your Records On." Going on this trip alone gave me time to think, time to dream, time to reflect, and time to ask and answer some hard questions for myself.

Each one of these were soul-enriching, life-changing, memory-making experiences for me.

Where is *your* Italy? It could be a beach or lake not too far from you. It could be sitting on your balcony or your back porch with a cup of coffee early in the morning before the day gets started.

It could be taking a walk or doing yoga. It could be sitting in a pew at your church during the middle of the week when no one is there. It could be reading a book in your sun room or taking a hot bath with a glass of wine at night. When you need to get still, it's time to recognize it and find your Italy.

Now there will be people that will be buzz-killers in our quest for pause. Unfortunately, it's such a foreign concept to most of us in the United States, and you might get bestowed the label "selfish" or "indulgent." While I was there, I had people who texted me about traveling to Italy by myself. I received the following messages while there.

"I could never do that."

"You're so brave."

"I'm sorry for you."

"I didn't think you'd actually do it."

I understood what was happening: people were projecting their own fears onto me. Being alone—traveling alone—terrifies most people, particularly women who are social creatures by nature. But being alone—as scary as it is—is important to self-discovery. It's important to be alone so that you are able to hear your own voice.

> It's important to be alone so that you are able to hear your own voice.

Sharon Pope

Life Lessons in Truth

When I was in Italy, in between spas, I also spent a few days in Florence, which you read a little about in another chapter. While there, I visited the majestic Duomo, and they happened to be holding a Catholic mass in English late one afternoon. I attended that service, and there was a familiar prayer from all the years of growing up Catholic that brought me to tears that afternoon thousands of miles from home:

Lamb of God, you take away the sins of the world, have mercy on us.
Lamb of God, you take away the sins of the world, have mercy on us.
Lamb of God, you take away the sins of the world, grant us peace.

There's a story that was told to me by a dear friend. (I may get these details a bit wrong, but you'll get the point.) It's a biblical story that explains why whenever we see an image of God carrying a sheep, its legs are typically wrapped in bandages. It is said that if a lamb ran away from its flock, the master would break its legs. The master would carry the lamb everywhere and care for it while it healed, so that it would learn to trust in the grace of its master, to know that if it stays with its flock, it will be protected, and never run away again.

During my trip to Italy, I had some wounded limbs that required healing. I placed myself in God's loving care during that trip, and He helped me heal some of those broken places and provided me the ability to forgive myself. It was during that trip that I found and valued the presence of peace in my life. And I'll never stray away again.

CHAPTER 26

Bubble Wrap

I always wonder why birds stay in the same place when they can fly anywhere on earth. Then I ask myself the same question.
—Harun Yahya

I was brought up in a relatively safe, predictable home environment. I lived with my mom, dad, and older brother. My brother and I fought too much, as kids will do (although we were particularly bad); we always lived in a small suburban home, attended church every week, and moved every three to four years as a result of my dad's job. Moving that often can lead to an unpredictable life, but when it's done with that much regularity and expectation, it's actually surprising how undisruptive I remember it being.

I believe it was my role as I moved into adulthood to then create my own safe, stable, secure life. What I created was a shell, a cocoon, or what I affectionately call a life in bubble wrap.

I think many of us do this instinctively. We stay in our jobs collecting a 0–3 percent annual increase with fewer and more expensive benefits, smaller workspaces, shorter deadlines, and greater stress. It's just how it is; it's part of the deal, and although we don't like it, we feel powerless to do anything about it. We try to save a little money for that eventual rainy day or retirement, but it's difficult. Some of us stay with our partner, not because we're happy, but because we're not unhappy enough to change.

I've actually heard people say that they're staying in their current relationship only because the thought of having to go out, find someone new, and go through the whole dating process again is far too daunting. Some stay in their roles at work because the thought of updating their résumé, applying for positions, and interviewing is too overwhelming. Some people stay in this cycle because it feels secure, albeit monotonous. Some people stay because they don't think that they could do any better. Some people stay in this cycle because they believe that this is all there is, that this is what life's all about. And when we look around and so many others are living a similar sort of life, there's a certain comfort in that.

We want to move somewhere warmer or cooler or sunnier or somewhere we can enjoy all four seasons. We want to live somewhere by the water or in the mountains—yet most of us never do. I've gone on vacations and mentally toyed with the idea of living a far simpler life in that destination. It is on those vacations that I inevitably meet people who have actually done that. They've sold their suburban home, quit their jobs, and sold their belongings to move to an island; they bought a boat and some insurance and now give parasailing trips to tourists on the ocean all day, every day. Who does that? Who has that kind of courage or vision or sheer carelessness to uproot their lives and all that they know, leaving behind family and friends and all the things we take comfort in: the same route to work each day, the same home we've lived in for decades, our routine.

A sense of security in our homes, in our jobs, in our relationships, and in our lives gives us comfort. But what if being truly safe doesn't really exist?

The sweet couple who for years have cleaned my home had their car broken into while they were in church.

Some incredibly bright, competent people have been released from their jobs. No job is safe or guaranteed.

Relationships evolve and change; I don't have many of the same friends I had only a few short years ago.

People who thought they could depend on their savings, pensions, or Social Security to support themselves after their working years are finding that it's not enough.

Families faithfully paying their mortgages lose their homes when they're suddenly hit with insurmountable medical bills when Dad became sick.

Fear may be a liar—but so is the illusion of safety.

> Fear may be a liar—but so is the illusion of safety.

Change is incredibly difficult for most people, so we don't exactly seek it out. When it's forced upon us, we fumble through it until we can find our way back to the stable and secure place we crave. But it's just so much easier to stay with the status quo and continue to do what we've always done than it is to create that change we'd like to see for ourselves, the kind of life that lives only in our imaginations. It's infinitely more difficult to do any more than imagine and play with those dreams we have inside of us. What's that saying about an object in motion stays in motion and an object at rest ...?

Anyway, that comfort, that routine, that repetition is all "bubble wrap." It makes us feel like we're safe and secure, but it has its own set of dangers—for one, it can suffocate us. Bubble wrap makes us complacent, making it difficult to move and bend, stretch and grow. Bubble wrap holds us tightly where we are today and doesn't allow us to take that next step into our future or follow a new calling or pursue a new desire or take a new risk.

Life Lessons in Truth

Bubble wrap can be a good thing at certain times in our lives, such as after a death or difficult period of time where some healing is needed. I also think some people genuinely like it there, so they're not going to seek otherwise, and that's okay. (However, I'm guessing since you're reading this book that you're not one of those people.) Then there are those of us that need to be able to grow, to create and to follow our dreams. It is for us, then, that bubble wrap can be more harmful than helpful.

I have found that those seemingly safe, secure, stagnant routines are a dangerous place for me to live. I need to keep growing and learning—in my faith, in my profession, in my relationships, in my life, in order to feel alive. I have held the soul-crushing jobs in corporate America, I have had the numbing marriage and the false friendships. I needed to submerge myself in something that I was passionate about—I had tried several things before—but none of them worked either. Turns out, what I really needed was to embark on the journey to find my authentic self—and let me tell you there was no bubble wrap supplied on that endeavor and I lived to tell about it.

CHAPTER 27

Enlightenment

You are a child of God. Your playing small does not serve the world. There is nothing enlightening about shrinking so that other people won't feel unsure around you.
—Marianne Williamson, *A Return to Love*

Enlightenment is one of those elusive qualities that is almost like water through our hands: once we think we've got it, it falls away. Although the word itself probably makes us think of philosophers, intellectuals, crystals, and hippies, I like to think of it as an awakening.

To become more enlightened, we go on this endless transformative, personal journey that is sometimes dangerous, sometimes uplifting, always challenging; this journey always has stops along the way with real truth, real feelings, and real personal growth. It's not really completely attainable. There is no finish line. There is no degree, graduation day, or certificate of accomplishment. It's certainly not something on your "to-do" list that once completed never needs revisiting. I don't know what it looks like to be truly, completely enlightened, because to me, it's something that I strive for and gain a deeper understanding of over time but never really fully attain.

> To become more enlightened, you go on this endless transformative, personal journey that is sometime dangerous, sometimes uplifting, always challenging; this journey always has stops along the way with real truth, real feelings, and real personal growth.

In its most basic form, I think of it as self-awareness. It's the awareness that all the questions we have in our lives begin and end with us. We begin to understand our personalities, our characters, our wants, needs, desires, goals, and dreams, our beliefs, fears, and shortcomings. If we know any of those things about ourselves, I think we have earned the right to consider ourselves "enlightened." Know that most human beings will live their whole lives without being able to recognize, understand, or articulate those characteristics that make up the core of who they are. So, if you're able to do that, you're a rock star and pretty darn advanced along this journey.

When we are self-aware, we are able to articulate our purpose on this earth. We know the answers to these questions: *What is my true purpose in life? What was I created to do? Why am I here? What are my gifts? What legacy will I leave?*

I believe I was placed on this earth as a healer to "speak faith into people." Don't be scared ... I'm not talking about going door to door, preaching and forcing my beliefs on you, hoping that you're lost enough to grab this life raft because it happened to come along. No, I believe that I was placed on this earth, in people's lives at this particular moment to encourage them to see themselves as greater than they can see for themselves, so that they can accomplish more than they thought they could, to help them understand their innermost truths and tap into their own innate wisdom to seek out what they deserve and not settle for mediocrity in any part of their lives. I believe that every experience I have in life holds a purpose, and I know that I haven't walked through the fire for no good reason. Nor was that blaze just set for me and my own personal growth alone. That fire was meant to bring heat to others in the cold. That's what I know about myself. That is my gift. That was my lesson. That's what brings me joy. That is my light. And that is no accident.

Life Lessons in Truth

This path ... it's not easy and there aren't shortcuts. It takes tremendous courage to look into our own souls, to be brutally honest about what drives us, what brings us joy, and what causes us pain. It takes the strength to walk away from those things and people that no longer serve us; those that steal energy or dim our light. It takes a degree of peace to allow ourselves to feel emotions without drowning in them. What most of us find on that journey is some of our own demons have held us down, have given us false security, or have fed our egos for so long and are so familiar that we should be able to call them by name.

Not everyone will be ready or equipped to see what lies in their shadows—and that's okay. As a matter of fact, there will be times that the path to enlightenment brings to the surface some painful or scary anxieties that we're not prepared to deal with at that particular time. That's okay—it's not the right time. Be gentle. Shining a light in a dark place usually sends things running for cover; it's no different with us and our light.

Also understand that this self-exploration that we're on will scare some other people—friends, family—because it will bring to the surface some of their own insecurities. They will see and experience us overcoming some things they may need to deal with themselves. So that may frighten them. That's okay; just recognize it for what it is without judgment and keep moving on your path, giving them the space they require as they handle their own fear.

Some people in my life that had been friends with me for years, and even some family, found it easier to unplug from me than to take the time to understand what was happening to me. I made some decisions that were probably irrational financially at the time, just to remove myself physically from the toxic environment in which I was living. To some people, that didn't make sense. People wondered why in the world I completely renovated and then sold that big, pretty house with a yard. Others wouldn't discuss what had happened to my marriage for fear that it would bring to the surface the reality and unhappiness of their own. For some it was just easier to judge me, making up stories in their heads about the kind of person they thought I had become. Even when it's disguised as hate, understand that it's only fear digging in. It's just fear; and they just haven't realized yet, as you have, that fear is a liar.

In its greatest achievable form, I view enlightenment as the highest level of knowledge, acceptance, and love for who we are at this moment in time. It's never really attained, because we're always changing and growing as individuals, and we need a renewed amount of grace each and every day. We're always learning to hold ourselves and our beliefs a little lighter and love ourselves a little more. No one, ourselves included, benefits from us denying or burying who we are and who we were meant to be. When we find our light, we need to share it; gifts weren't made to be kept to ourselves; gifts by their very nature are created to be given away.

CHAPTER 28

Faith

Faith is believing what we do not see. The reward of faith is to see what we believe.
—Augustine

We cannot have both faith and doubt at the exact same time. We cannot have faith and fear at the same time. They are opposing, intangible emotions, and if we have an ounce of doubt or fear about something, then we do not have faith. It's one or the other. And there will be times when we need to choose which one we will embrace.

When we place our bets on multiple combinations, we're gambling and that comes from a place of doubt. Hanging onto one boyfriend that we know won't last, even as we're moving into another, new relationship is placing our bets. God forbid we be alone for even a minute. So we want to make sure the new relationship is really as promising as we hope it is before we let the existing boyfriend off the hook. That's not showing faith in ourselves or in the new boyfriend.

Having a "plan B" in our chosen profession also begins from a place of doubt. Maybe we've graduated college as a music major and all we've ever known and loved in our life is music. So why in the world did we listen to our parents when they told us to get a double major in accounting so that we would have something to fall back on in case "that music thing" didn't work out?

If we had absolute, unwavering faith in who we were, whom we wanted in our lives, and the direction we were headed, we wouldn't play the odds or have a backup plan. So, if we have a plan B (or C, D, E, or Z) in any part of our lives right now, we should explore that a bit to understand why. We should explore what's driving that and what would it take for us to have faith and rid ourselves of all doubt.

Over the years and through my journey, I've grown in my faith: faith in myself (that I really am strong), faith in that little voice inside me (that sometimes isn't so little), faith in the healing process (it cannot be ignored), and faith in God's plan for my life. For years I've had in the back of my mind that one day, maybe in another life, I would be an author and public speaker. I assumed that would be after retiring from corporate America when I wanted a slower pace, and I guess I always assumed that I would speak about leadership or motivation or women in business or some other corporate, boring, me-too–type topic. That's as far as I had ever got with that dream.

What began as an extension of journaling to lessen the pain and gain some clarity during a very difficult time in my life post-divorce were the beginnings of this book. Once I began thinking of it as a product, rather than just an outlet, I was writing it from a place of monetization; what would sell? what would get into the big bookstores? what would be commercially viable? ... as opposed to what was worthy of writing and what was worth reading. I certainly wasn't going to mention God in this book—after all, I would never get hired to come speak in a Fortune 500 company by talking about God. (This, by the way, was fine with me, because I have never been comfortable talking about my faith—ever.)

During the next major iteration of the book (I've rewritten this countless times), I knew I had to talk about God in the context of my journey, so I rewrote the introduction and included something akin to an "apology" for including references to God—because my story simply couldn't be told without Him.

By this last major rewrite, God's presence in my life was so profound and so impactful that I just went wherever He took me. I wrote what I was feeling. I wrote from a very private, but very authentic, place. I wrote as if I were writing for Him. And as you know by now, my faith story and beliefs about God at work in my life are woven throughout this book.

I grew up Catholic. I went to a Catholic school through the fourth grade. I was baptized as a baby, made my first Communion in grade school, attended classes, and then completed my confirmation as a young teenager. Virtually my entire family—on both my mother's and father's sides—was Catholic. We went to church every Sunday, or Saturday night, for a forty-five-minute mass. You shook people's hands in the middle of the mass, but you didn't really know anyone in the church; it was always too big to know people or make friends. You stood up, sat down, knelt, and recited the prayer along with the rest of the congregation. You didn't really read the Bible or talk about your faith. It wasn't something to be discussed or debated or explored. It was doctrine; there was one way to interpret God's teachings, and that was what we knew.

God is all too familiar with the fact that I've been completely uncomfortable talking about my faith my entire life, so I think in the midst of this He's getting a good chuckle. He is giving me the courage I need to do this. He knows I need constant support and reinforcement, and so He presents that to me in a form that I will see and understand. But, most of all, He gives me the peace in my heart that I need to keep going and following the path to wherever He's guiding me. The minute I start to let doubt in, I know that I'm showing God that I no longer have faith in Him or His plan—so that doubt doesn't really stand a chance. It might visit, but it never takes its coat off and stays. I no longer worry, because there's nothing to worry about. I don't try to control, because it would do me no good.

The peace God has placed in my heart also gives me:

- strength when old colleagues look at me like I've lost my mind as I attempt to explain the transition I'm making from chief marketing officer to author, public speaker, and life coach (asking, "What in the world is a life coach?");

- tolerance when family and friends try to be supportive but always end up saying something thoughtless that shows me they really don't understand;

- understanding that He wouldn't have placed this desire in my heart, He wouldn't have given me the skills, just to then watch me fail; and

- power over my own happiness.

Life Lessons in Truth

In the context of this massive career change, and emerging out of a pretty difficult time in my life, I knew that the only thing of any value that I could give to anyone was my time and a piece of myself. And, if all I had to give was myself, then I knew I needed to get better. I needed to flex some new muscles, grow in my understanding of the healing process through experience, and acquire some training that would expand my knowledge. If I didn't get better, I wouldn't be able to help as many people.

So, one night when I was just too tired to write but knew I needed to work, I began doing some online research. It had occurred to me that I should look into coaching earlier that day when I heard a happiness coach being interviewed on the radio. I thought, "What in the world is a happiness coach?" The happiness coach idea didn't quite feel right for me, so my Internet search led me to life coaching classes. I researched several programs and came across one training program in particular that I became really excited about. I mean, I was inspired! It was one of those times that I could actually feel my heart yell "yes!" because it just felt right. This course wasn't insignificant; it was a nine-month commitment and $7,000—during a time when I was not actively employed—but it felt right, and I trusted the journey and my own inner wisdom. So, I went to enroll in this nine-month certification program and found out that the next class set to begin in a few weeks was sold out. The next opportunity to begin might be four months away. Well, that sure did burst my bubble. Have you ever been so excited about something that you wanted it to start right away? You didn't want to be patient, you didn't want to do more research, you didn't want to wait to begin creating a future for yourself that you were excited about right now? That was me. So, that night before I went to bed, I sent the course organizer an e-mail expressing my excitement, even offering to pay more if necessary. This was out of character for me, because I am a notorious, self-proclaimed, and currently recovering law-abiding, etiquette-loving, rule-follower.

But here's the thing, you have to have faith before the miracle will occur. And I just knew this was the right step for me at this phase in my life.

You have to have faith before the miracle will occur.

I received a personalized e-mail back the following evening. It said that they had such a tremendous response to the course that they had decided earlier that day to open it up to another twenty-six participants. If I wanted to be in that class, I just had to be one of the first people to respond. Of course, I responded within the hour, and the rest is history. Three weeks later and $7,000 poorer, I began the training that would become an enormous catalyst for my future and give me that next step in the journey God was plotting for me. Once again, I knew He was at work. He just keeps presenting opportunities, and I just keep following where it takes me. These desires—writing, speaking, coaching—He placed those in my heart. I didn't place them there. I'm just listening and following.

Once in a while, when I take the time to describe this time in my life for people, they will ask me something like, "Why has God been working in your life?" or "Where has He been in my life?" The only answer I have is that He is working in all of our lives, I just happen to be listening and paying attention right now. That wasn't always the case for me. But I got to a point where I had to get still, where I had to heal, where I had to sit my ass down and just listen—for a long time—and trust where He would take me. What I found was that He was there and ready to help me become all that He has envisioned for my life.

I may no longer identify myself as "Catholic"; I don't know exactly what religion this all makes me, but I do know that I have a broad, deep, and open faith, and whatever it is, it just feels good.

CHAPTER 29

Angels

A fine glass vase goes from treasure to trash, the moment it is broken. Fortunately, something else happens to you and me. Pick up your pieces. Then, help me gather mine.
—Vera Nazarian, *The Perpetual Calendar of Inspiration*

Looking back on the most difficult times in my life, there is one thing that I am consistently, genuinely humbled by and grateful for. God surrounded me with the people that would save my life. He brought people to my side that were honest with me, strong when I needed them to be, loving confidants and warriors. Those people that stand by us in our time of need—those are our angels. Embrace them. Open up to them. Learn from them. Get to know them. Trust them. Love them back.

> Those people that reach out to us in our
> time of need—those are our angels.

It was a Sunday afternoon in the months during my separation. I was living in a small furnished apartment on the other side of town. Like many Sunday afternoons following my separation, I was crying, saddened by a broken heart. That day a dear friend who was also separated from her husband was there with me and said something to me that I will never forget. She said, "Don't you realize? You are the Daughter of the King. If you truly felt that, if you really believed it, how would you allow someone to treat you?" This. Stopped. Me. What she was telling me was true, but I didn't believe it. I didn't feel that I was worthy of that kind of love. But it was truth looking me right in the eye. That phrase has since guided my life—both professionally and personally. It has become the filter through which I live my life.

The gift she gave me that day has allowed me to experience people and situations differently: I treated myself better, I listened to and learned from the angels around me and found beauty in even difficult experiences.

I had the privilege of knowing a southern belle who was born in Louisiana, lived in Oklahoma City, and married my grandfather several years after his first wife, my grandmother Constance, had passed away. Nora Lee was an absolute angel to a grandfather who, although I did love him, could have easily been the most difficult man to love in the history of men. He bullied and degraded Nora Lee. He could be equal parts loving and, at the exact same time, insistent, insulting, and close-minded. He acted as though he were entitled and mistreated, but I believe my grandfather was really just deeply lonely and insecure. Nora Lee stood by him and supported him out of love and a deep belief in the institution of marriage, when so many others would have walked away and never looked back.

Nora Lee was one of the sweetest, kindest women that ever lived. Her first husband passed away when she was still relatively young. She spent all of her working years as a counselor for Weight Watchers. She was sentimental, keeping and sharing nearly every funny card or inspirational quote ever given to her; her smile was absolutely contagious. Many times, I found myself trying to protect her from my own blood relative, my grandfather. She was an angel in my life.

I visited her and my grandfather every year until my grandfather passed away. After Grandpa died, I never went back to Oklahoma until Nora Lee's funeral. I never went back just to spend time with her and tell her how much I loved her. I never tried to call her on the phone. I would think about her and had purchased cards for her that went unsent. She passed away and I found out at the funeral that she had asked her daughter about me the week prior to her passing.

At the time of her death, the plane tickets to get to Oklahoma City were outrageously expensive. So, I again was struggling with whether or not I should go, whether or not I deserved to go and pay my respects, since I felt so guilty about not remaining close to her. Another angel in my life said, "Let me make this easy for you." She picked up her cell phone to contact the airlines and, right then, cashed in her frequent flyer points so that I could get a deeply discounted plane ticket to attend Nora Lee's funeral. Just like that. In a matter of minutes, that decision was made, and I would be on the flight the next morning and back that same night. I think I will always remember that gift of clarity and grace she gave to me so that I can do the same for someone else someday.

One day, I was walking through a mall in a small town and wandered into a perfume store. I was waiting for someone, so I was literally just killing time, sort of absentmindedly browsing, with no intention to make a purchase. The saleswoman didn't approach me right away, paying attention to the other conversation that was happening in the store. After a while she and I chatted about the fragrances I liked. I told her I always have an extra bottle of Victor Rolf's Flowerbomb on hand and tried on several different Calvin Klein Euphoria fragrances.

It wasn't long before I was making a purchase, and she stopped to ask me, "Do you mind if I ask what you do?" I told her I was in marketing, because I was at the time. She shared with me that although she was in sales, she was feeling a pull to go back to school, to pursue either a psychology degree or nursing. She was wondering if it was too late, and whether at age twenty-one it might be too late to pursue her dreams. Mind you, I was forty-one, and I was still talking about what I would do differently if I had it to do all again.

What was amazing was that this complete stranger felt the pull to confide in me and seek advice in her life. She didn't know me. I walked into that store to kill time waiting for a friend and walked out filled with so much joy to have connected with someone, having been given the opportunity to help someone else's journey. What an amazing gift she gave me that day; she reaffirmed my calling in this world and instilled the belief in me that it wasn't too late for either of us.

When I decided to try something new and start my own business, it was remarkable how God surrounded me with people who had faith and confidence in me, believing in my gifts and talents and encouraging me to find a way to make a living doing what I loved. I would share my ideas with one friend, and she would help me build on those ideas to create something even better. Another friend would inspire me by sharing the dreams she had for her future. And another friend saw in me what was possible (before I had ever told her my ideas) and gave me the confidence and courage to follow my heart. When I wanted to publish this book, I had friends who read it multiple times and gave me the gift of their honest feedback to make it better.

I have been surrounded by so many inspiring and courageous people that I've had the privilege of knowing and learning from:

Friend and business executive Mike Sayre taught me the importance of having the right attitude. There will be times where people will be taking your lead, reacting to a particular situation—they will mimic your reaction, so make sure you're letting them see the right one.

From my friend, author and personal endurance trainer, Ironman Tim Barrett, I've learned that to be a great writer, you have to be disciplined in your approach. It requires you to sit down for several hours every day to write, in the same spot, around the same time each day. Just like endurance training, there will be days that you won't feel like doing it—but you need to write anyway so that you keep those muscles strong. Most of it may never get read, but without that discipline, none of it will ever get read. (From his lovely wife, Lisa, I learned about one of my favorite wines, Chateau Montelena.)

My friend and neighbor Jenny Schneider showed me that there is so much beauty and grace in caring for someone in their final years. I've been fortunate to be a witness to the respectful and joy-filled life she shares with her aging mother.

From my friend, entrepreneur, author, motivator, and personal trainer Sue Markovitch, I've learned that life is too short: face your fears, follow your dreams, respect your body, find your strength, and live with unabashed, unapologetic, unwavering joy.

From my former pastor and second father, Grayson Atha, I learned that everyone is a child of God. Period. Everyone—even those (especially those!) who are different from you.

Tracey Carruthers, an author and executive coach (I also like to think of her as my own personal Maya Angelou), taught me two very important lessons. The first is "You cannot separate the human experience from the business experience," which means that if you're not healthy in your personal life, you won't be healthy and productive in your work life either. She also taught me to trust my own intuition: "You know truth when you feel it."

Antonio Smith, former collegiate and professional football player, current mechanical engineer, sports commentator, community leader, public speaker and philanthropist, has become a dear friend of mine. Antonio grew up in poverty and had a lot of people in his life that doubted he would ever become anything. His life story taught me and so many others to never let the fear of failure keep you from doing what you really want to do and all that you are capable of achieving.

I used to have a woman in my life that I referred to as my "bonus mom," but others called her Donna. She used to say that the most important day throughout the year was your birthday, because it was the day you changed the world. You changed the world for your parents and your family, and the world, in turn, has since felt the ripple of your presence.

From Derrick I've learned that you really can leave something that's troubling you at God's feet and rest your mind knowing that it's being handled.

I have had people I could call upon and count on, people who challenge me and stretch me, and most importantly, angels whom I adore and trust, because these people in many ways, at various times and to varying degrees, saved me.

Life Lessons in Truth

We're not meant to do this alone. This thing called life can become difficult, so we need people along the way to stand beside us. The journey to an authentic life is not without its challenges. Who are your angels? Would you recognize them? Would you let them in? Open your eyes, expose your heart, listen for guidance. Share your stories and your dreams with others, and just watch what happens. God and the universe will bring you exactly what you need. Look for truth, pray for peace, but expect miracles.

CHAPTER 30

Authenticity

Take time to recognize that there are things going on within you that need to be felt, or said, or lived, or grieved ... Pay attention to the authentic self. Now about the word authentic. It is related to the word author and you can think of it as being the author of your own self. When you're living your own reality, you become the sovereign of your own life. You know who you are.
—Marion Woodman, *The Power of the Feminine*

At this point in the book, I'm hoping you've had some time to do some searching within your own soul. I hope you've been able to draw out a renewed vision of yourself into the light—one that feels right, is happy, and has some peace, one you can call your own. You've likely identified some things you need to heal, and I hope you have the reassurance that even though you don't know exactly where your path will take you, you'll be okay.

Living authentically is not exactly a destination. It's okay to not know where you will land, because life is a process; healing is a process; growth and change is a process. Sometimes it's just hard work—but I can assure you that getting committed to finding a life that is your own is worth it.

Getting committed to finding a life that is your own is worth it.

We all have this image in our minds of what happiness will look like for each of us. Forget about that picture for a bit, and just trust the process and the path you're on. If you are the author of your own life, how do you want to live? How do you want to experience each day? How do you want others to experience you? What will be your contribution? There are no limits; there are no more lies.

Life Lessons in Truth

When we're living authentically, we connect to our own truth and the wisdom within our souls. Sometimes that truth carries with it some weight. It's not all light and superficial and carefree. Our truth may not ring true for someone else, and we need to have enough respect for one another as human beings to allow for those differences.

Although everyone's version of an authentic life is as unique as they are,

> I think living authentically means knowing who you are and who you are not and being madly in love with that person;
>
> I think it means you've had some experiences in life that have knocked you back or even knocked you down, but you are able to heal, while gaining wisdom and strength in the process;
>
> I think living authentically means not allowing other voices to drown out your own voice;
>
> I think it means you've forgiven: yourself and everyone else;
>
> I think it means you've come to trust in the ebb and flow of life. You trust God's plan in your life; and you trust that there are angels that come into your life just when you need them and experiences that occur so that you can gain the learning that you need at that particular moment.

For me, living an authentic life means there's an openness to my heart that wasn't there before. I let people in. I share it. I nourish it and love it a bit more each day.

Epilogue

In order for me to truly live an authentic life, I had to look truth in the eye and become painfully self-aware. I am a child of God, first and foremost. I am a sinner. I am a teacher and a coach. I am as generous as I am loyal. I am the ultimate multitasker and hard worker, smart, capable and confident, able to achieve a lot in my life and my career. I have found a great deal of joy and meaning in just being still. I want to always be learning and growing. I want to have fewer "things" in my life, but more meaningful experiences. I love hard. I feel deeply. I can be vulnerable, trusting, and open. In the marathon of life, I have been blessed to be surrounded by a blanket of positive, uplifting, soulful people, and for that, I will be forever grateful. I am beautiful, inside and out. I am loved, and I am worthy of that love in my life. I am imperfect and a continuous work in progress. I am all these things and a few more.

In case you still need it, please allow this book to give you permission to find happiness in your life. A soul sister of mine, Traci, recently shared her belief with me: "We all have the God-given right to be happy." I think she's right. I do and so do you. It does not matter what we've done; it doesn't matter what we've experienced or endured. Because for all of those misdeeds, there is grace, and for all those pains, there is forgiveness.

I remember the last meal I had with my ex-husband. We were at a small restaurant with another couple we were visiting in Michigan. The restaurant was in an old house, and we were sitting upstairs in a small room where there were only about three other tables. The home had a Victorian style with tables covered in an older, damask-patterned vinyl tablecloth, and the walls were lined with floral wallpaper. My husband and friends all seemed to have a great deal to talk about, but I wasn't really listening. I remember being very distracted by a piece of artwork on the wall, which I've since learned is called *The Hardest of Easy Choices,* by Rodney White. Some of the letters to the phrase are cut off so that it's not so literal, but it is easy to decipher what it says.

Along this journey, there are many choices that we make daily. We make the choice to pursue a life filled with happiness. We make the choice to learn from our mistakes. We make the choice to face our fears and call them by name. We make the difficult choice to stop blaming others and forgive their imperfections. We also make the even more difficult choice to stop blaming and start forgiving ourselves. Forgiveness doesn't mean it didn't matter or that it didn't hurt; but forgiveness does allow us to simultaneously acknowledge the pain and release it.

Another important choice we have on our path to healing is to choose to live a grateful life. This very simple choice has never once failed me. It has followed me through every aspect of my life, through all the tears, all the years, all the lies, all the hurt; and without fail, gratitude has always led me to joy. When I'm experiencing something simple and beautiful, that experience is enlarged through gratitude and presence. When I'm going through something difficult, I can still be grateful for the lesson. Even when I'm hurting, I can be thankful for my ability to feel and experience the emotion, knowing that it will pass and I will be okay.

Some days it is enough to just be grateful for this one moment. When I recognize all the blessings I have in my life—in that one moment, I have a little more peace and a little more joy. When I think about the people God has placed in my life, I am humbled by the way they demonstrate to me an open heart, a sweet soul, a deep love, a strong faith. They become one of my many teachers; some are my angels.

These days my prayer is some version of "thank you." *Thank You, Lord, for the abundance of blessings You've given me. Thank You for all the love and light and angels I have in my life—those I've met, as well as those whose paths I have yet to cross. Thank You, most of all, for continuing to be present and at work in my life. In all I do, in all I am, my only goal is to honor You and the plan You have for me. Amen.*